Potworks

Published by the Royal Commission on the Historical Monuments of England,
Fortress House, 23 Savile Row, London W1X 2JQ

© Royal Commission on the Historical Monuments of England 1991

First published 1991

ISBN 1 873592 01 9

British Library Cataloguing in Publication Data
A CIP catalogue record for this book is available from the British Library

Designed by Chuck Goodwin, Lampada

Printed in Great Britain by BAS Printers Ltd, Stockbridge

Potworks

THE INDUSTRIAL ARCHITECTURE OF THE STAFFORDSHIRE POTTERIES

Diane Baker

ROYAL COMMISSION ON THE HISTORICAL MONUMENTS OF ENGLAND

CONTENTS

ILLUSTRATIONS

Plates

Figures

Maps

The author and publisher wish to thank the following for permission to reproduce illustrations:

Albion Galleries, Hanley (Plate 68); Birmingham Central Reference Library (Boulton and Watt Collection) (Plates 20, 42); Mr G Godden (Plates 52, 53); University of Keele Library (Warrillow Collection) (Plates 23, 26, 27, 30, 90); Mr J Moorcroft (Plate 85); Mr D Morris (Plates 88, 93 – photographs now in the collection of the City of Stoke Museum and Art Gallery); William Salt Library, Stafford (Plates 1, 3); Spode, Stoke-on-Trent (Plate 49); the City of Stoke Museum and Art Gallery (Plates 7, 10, 14, 17, 18, 28, 50, 83, 84, 89, 97); Mrs A I Vickers (Plate 73); and the Trustees of the Wedgwood Museum, Barlaston, Staffordshire (Plates 2, 8, 9, 11, 13, 19, 21, 94, 95).

CHAIRMAN'S FOREWORD

The Royal Commission on the Historical Monuments of England is delighted to be associated with the Stoke-on-Trent City Museum and Art Gallery in the publication of this volume on the potworks of the six towns which comprise the Potteries, the centre of the ceramic industry in England. This fruitful collaboration, dating from 1984, has underlined the Royal Commission's commitment to recording and publishing the rapidly vanishing monuments of our industrial heritage.

The genesis of the project is described in the author's preface, where all those who contributed to the final text are fully acknowledged. Commissioners would wish particularly to echo Diane Baker's thanks to the firms and householders who willingly allowed access to their properties, since without their help there would not be a book. We hope that the appearance of this volume will compensate owners for any inconvenience caused during the course of the work, as well as providing a timely reminder of the remarkable achievements of their forebears who gave this once sulphurous area its singular character.

PARK OF MONMOUTH

AUTHOR'S PREFACE AND ACKNOWLEDGEMENTS

This study is based on the work of the Stoke-on-Trent Historic Buildings Survey, carried out at the City Museum and Art Gallery between 1982 and 1985 under the auspices of the Manpower Services Commission (MSC) and the City Council. The Survey, initiated by Dr Cameron Hawke-Smith, Keeper of Archaeology at the City Museum and Art Gallery, and supervised by Andrew Dobraszczyc, included a team of approximately twenty workers each year.

The Survey set out to create a non-intensive record of all surviving buildings, dating from before 1924, within the present boundaries of the city. One hundred and twenty of these, selected to provide a representative sample illustrative of the principal types of building found in the area, were then recorded in greater detail. The potworks represent one part of this survey. All the records, comprising drawings, photographs and historical abstracts, are held as a permanent archive at the City Museum. A copy of the archive is also housed in the National Buildings Record at the Royal Commission on the Historical Monuments of England.

The Royal Commission on the Historical Monuments of England (RCHME) was approached in 1984 for assistance in producing a publication based on the work of the Survey. In 1986, following the ending of MSC support, the RCHME assumed responsibility for the funding of the publication. Since that time, the management of the project has been the responsibility of a Steering Committee, comprising Commissioners and staff of the RCHME and representatives of Stoke-on-Trent City Council.

In addition to financial assistance, the RCHME has undertaken the photography of buildings illustrated in the book (unless otherwise stated), redrawn the measured surveys for publication and taken responsibility for all editing and design work.

A large number of people have worked on the initial survey and on the preparation of the volume. I am particularly indebted to Dr Hawke-Smith and Andrew Dobraszczyc for their contribution throughout the course of the project; to Professor Maurice Beresford and Professor R A Buchanan, RCHME Commissioners, for their work on the Steering Committee; to Mr J T Smith for supervising the joint project in its early stages and to Dr Robin Thornes for supervising the academic aspects of this publication. Thanks are due also to: Robert Hook for undertaking additional survey work and preparing the measured drawings for publication; John Morrey for preparing the maps; Anthony Perry for taking the photographs; James Darwin for additional research; Davina Turner and Jean Irving for typing the drafts; Kate Owen and Rosalind Woodhouse for editorial guidance; Kirsty Cook for co-ordination of design and production; and, outside the Commission, Mrs Susan Whimster for her final editing of the text.

Grateful thanks are extended to all who worked on the Historic Buildings Survey and to all who assisted in the research for this volume: Pat Halfpenny, Ceramics Department, Stoke-on-Trent City Museum and Art Gallery; Gaye Blake Roberts and Lyn Miller, the Wedgwood Museum, Barlaston; Martin Philips, Keele University Library; Robert Copeland, Spode; Roy Smith, the Duchy of Lancaster; the staff at the Etruscan Bone Mill, Etruria, Gladstone Pottery Museum, Longton, Horace Barks Reference Library, Hanley, Stafford County Record Office, William Salt Library, Stafford, and the British Ceramic Research Association Library; and the staff at the Joint Diocesan Records Office, Lichfield, the Birmingham Reference Library archive and the Public Record Office in Chancery Lane and Kew.

Finally, I wish to thank all those firms and householders who gave their co-operation in allowing access to their properties. Special thanks are due to Burgess and Leigh Ltd, J Moorcroft Ltd, Aynsley China Ltd and Mason's Ironstone Ltd for the inconvenience caused by lengthy factory surveys during working hours.

Diane Baker

INTRODUCTION

The six towns of Burslem, Hanley, Stoke, Longton, Tunstall and Fenton make up what J B Priestley described as the 'mythical' City of Stoke-on-Trent. Collectively known as the Potteries, each of the towns had a quite distinct origin and they were only pressed into a loose association by reason of their common industries. For most people the district is best known from the novels, or television adaptations of the novels, of Arnold Bennett: by calling them the 'Five Towns' he added yet more confusion to the nomenclature. Somehow this confusion seems to fit the place. We no sooner seem to have it in focus than it shifts about and the patterns dissolve in chaos.

Industry made the place and at the root of the industries lie coal, iron and clay. In the early days iron dominated, but the district lost out to other parts of the country as its supplies of wood for fuel were exhausted. Although coal was to be had in abundance, the more accessible seams were not well suited to the smelting and casting of iron. But they were ideal for potting. A flourishing craft, using the local clays, sprang up in the backyards of Burslem yeoman farmers. By the mid eighteenth century, ceramics were so dominant that the district had become known nationally as the Potteries. By this time the local clays had already been replaced by imports from Devon and Cornwall. Today, the ceramic industry still remains supreme, but coal as fuel has in turn been replaced by gas and electricity and it is the skills of the pottery workers rather than the existence of raw materials that keeps the industry here.

The industrial development was accompanied by a steep rise in population. But, like many new centres of population owing their existence or expansion to the Industrial Revolution, the pottery towns gained formal recognition only slowly. Until the Reform Act of 1832 there was no direct parliamentary representation: legal identity as boroughs and urban districts was reluctantly conceded only at various dates between 1857 and 1894. This was one hundred years or more after the individual towns had unofficially declared their autonomy by the symbolic act of building town halls and markets.

Having at long last gained legal status, the six towns wore themselves out in a bitter conflict over the question of unification. The paralysis of indecision was brought to an end only when administrative unity was thrust on the towns in the strangely named Federation of 1910. Fifteen years later, as a belated recognition of its size and economic importance, Stoke-on-Trent, as the conurbation had become known, was granted the status of a city.

For Nikolaus Pevsner, Stoke-on-Trent was an 'urban tragedy'.[1] His verdict of 1974 was one of many unflattering comments on the City made during the last hundred years. For the outsider the problems start with the tangle of nomenclature: the next problem is one of orientation. There is no obvious centre for the whole. The town of Stoke nominally remains the administrative base, but the commercial and professional centre is Hanley. For many of the inhabitants, the City of Stoke-on-Trent is indeed mythical: they identify with their local town and many find few occasions to visit the other towns comprising the City. If this were not confusion enough, there is also the physical conjunction with Newcastle under Lyme, a medieval borough which remains jealously independent of its overgrown upstart neighbour.

Whatever our views of Stoke-on-Trent's urban messiness, the historical processes by which it came about are of the greatest interest. The physical structure of the place embodies its social and industrial history. Very few surviving buildings go back before 1800 and yet it is to the eighteenth and seventeenth centuries, and before, that we must look for the origins of the industries that came to maturity in the nineteenth century. We must look even further back, to medieval times and beyond, for the origins of the communities and the patterns of landownership and mineral rights that were still having a controlling influence in the nineteenth century. The earlier settlements from which the towns grew, directly or indirectly, were based on subsistence farming. Coal and clay were hardly relevant to the earlier way of life, though the heavy, poorly drained soils they produced were not favourable to cereal-growing. The medieval landscape was one of small pastoral enclosures, broad meandering mud tracks and extensive woodlands and commons. Quarrying, iron-working, charcoal-burning, potting – all these activities flourished as a supplement to livestock farming. Although traditional open fields are known to have existed, the system was probably never very firmly entrenched and it was abandoned almost everywhere at an early date.

This was a landscape and a society that was marginal to the established agricultural economy. Until its mineral resources began to be tapped systematically it remained poor and neglected. Although it occupied a central position in England, it was always a backwater. The nearest navigable rivers were some thirty miles away. It lay a few miles off the major thoroughfares linking London and the north west and its roads were no more than a series of drovers' tracks bypassing the tollgates of Newcastle under Lyme. Agriculturally, it was negligible.

This landscape and the way of life it generated are the essential background to the later industrialisation. The yeoman-farmer families of the sixteenth and seventeenth centuries, being free of the strait-jacket of the open-field system, enjoyed an almost complete freedom to sell, lease and mortgage their land. They were undoubtedly poor in comparison with their peers in the south and east of England, but they had economic independence. In this they were unlike their neighbours, the burgesses of Newcastle under Lyme, where the anachronism of the open-field system persisted until the nineteenth century. They were also free from interference by a jealous lord of the manor. The Duchy of Lancaster, which was lord of the manor for much of the Potteries, showed little interest in the district until the late eighteenth century, when the value of the minerals was becoming obvious. None of the lords of the manor cared much about the cottagers who built their tiny makeshift dwellings on roadside verges, commons and wastes. As in some other parts of the country, where the manor was in royal hands, leniency towards the lowest orders prevailed. On this ground the poor proliferated, shielded by seigneurial negligence from the pressures of improving landlords.

The wealthiest lived at a remove. Like the gods of Homer, they were virtually inaccessible, but their actions, often seemingly arbitrary, could have catastrophic effects for ordinary people. The wealthy families included the Sneyds, the Leveson-Gowers, the Foleys and the Parkers, and there are parallels in their family histories. They appeared first in the records as coal and iron-masters; they acquired their estates by purchase in the great property sales of the late sixteenth century; and most of them were elevated to the nobility in the eighteenth and nineteenth centuries.

The aristocracy remained interested in extractive industry through to the end of the nineteenth century. They were well placed to invest the capital needed for the exploitation of the deeper and more valuable deposits. The Foleys were instrumental in opening up the iron mines in the Normacot area of Longton and the furnace there was producing a significant proportion of Britain's pig iron by the end of the sixteenth century. The Leveson-Gowers acquired extensive interests in minerals in the south of the district through their purchase of the Trentham Estate; they also took up a lease on the mineral rights held by the Duchy of Lancaster in the Hanley area.

There was a great social gap below this aristocratic stratum and the local gentry, who chose to live, as often as not, on their estates of a few hundred acres or less, intermarrying with the more prosperous yeomanry. The gentry did not themselves stoop to trade, but they acted as guarantors, mortgagees and money-lenders for the rising class of small-scale entrepreneurs. Many of these families dwindled in the eighteenth century and their halls became ramshackle ruins, surviving incongruously amid streets of terraced houses.

Next below the gentry were the yeoman families. Sometimes helped up the social ladder by marriage connections with the lesser gentry, these families produced the landless younger sons who became the makers of the new industry. Perhaps the best known and best documented of these families were the Wedgwoods. They first appeared in Burslem in the late sixteenth century and rapidly proliferated, acquiring modest estates through marriage and some lucky bequests. During the seventeenth and early eighteenth century, several Wedgwoods became noted potters. By the time Josiah Wedgwood was apprenticed in 1744, the Wedgwoods were one of a cluster of manu-facturing families on the threshold of replacing the gentry as the leaders of local society.

Lastly, and at a marked distance below, were the cottagers and labourers, men of at most a few acres carved out of common land, who lived mainly by selling their labour. Though outside recognised 'society', and for that reason poorly documented, they were numerous, working as miners, iron-workers, potters and agricultural labourers. In the course of time they became the foundation of the industrial labouring class and some struggled through their own efforts towards the status of employers and manufacturers in their own right.

The first phase of the industrial development of the district can be taken as ending with the transport revolution of the mid eighteenth century. Until the turnpiking of the first road through part of the Potteries in 1759, none of the roads was suited to wheeled traffic. Clay and flints were brought in and pottery was carried out on the backs of animals and men – the cratesmen. The efforts of the potters to establish proper roads were resisted by the burgesses of Newcastle under Lyme: the stranglehold of the 'ancient borough' was only broken by an ingenious system of linkages connecting all the Potteries communities. Almost immediately afterwards, in 1766, the Trent and Mersey Canal was begun.

Whilst the road system had rescued the Potteries from total obscurity, the canal was to place it in the forefront of the national stage. It now became possible for the asset of the central position to be realised. Once the watershed of east and west-flowing rivers was breached by the Harecastle Tunnel, the Potteries had equal access to the American market via Liverpool and the European market via Hull. The effect on the industry and the society it supported can be described as revolutionary.

In the fifty years following the opening of the Trent and Mersey in 1777, the pottery towns emerged as urban centres. Burslem grew directly out of a medieval village in an orthodox manner. Hanley and Longton developed from a scatter of irregular and unauthorised cottage settlements on the waste. Fenton originated as a row of cottages alongside the main road, equidistant between the mother villages of Great and Little Fenton. Tunstall and Stoke were both planned, artificial communities, created through the initiative of local landowners and manufacturers. What is remarkable is that despite the variety of their origins, each of the communities followed a similar path towards civic identity. Each community assumed the effective status of an independent town at a very early stage, when its population numbered no more than a few thousands, and its civic efforts were then largely concentrated on preserving its separateness from its neighbours, the other pottery towns. This had disastrous long-term consequences for the Potteries as a whole, since it meant that the impetus towards the establishment of civic structures was fragmented. We can see this illustrated in the story of the thirteen town halls: the earliest town halls were replaced by grandiose buildings in the mid nineteenth century: these were replaced yet again, or enlarged, in the early twentieth century, as a threat of unification became more menacing. In fact, by the time these latest buildings were completed they were already redundant. The City of Stoke-on-Trent still has seven town halls (two in Burslem), monuments to this phase of municipal cussedness.

The industries of the Potteries were uniquely filthy and environmentally devastating. A permanent cloud of darkness hung over the place. In the heyday of the bottle oven, about two thousand kilns spewed out black smoke almost without stop. Sulphurous fumes were added to the inferno by the furnaces of the iron and steel industry. Buildings were blackened within a few years, and vegetation was blighted. There was no escape from the unhealthiness of the towns within the places of work: the dust of ground flint and bone and the poison of lead glazes ate into the life core of the people, so that a writer of 1908 declared: 'There are no old people here'.[2] To these hazards were added those of a landscape that was being systematically undermined from below and whose surface was pocked with vast precipitous quarries. Fissures were liable to open up in any house or street, causing dwellings to collapse. One individual disappeared without trace in the centre of Hanley when a disused pit gaped open without warning.

Now that the air over Stoke-on-Trent is as clean and sweet as any in Britain, and most of the slag heaps and quarries have been greened, it is possible to contemplate its surviving idiosyncratic architecture with detachment, even a certain nostalgia. In the years between 1982 and 1985, the new City Museum and Art Gallery, itself a monument to the continuing pride of the Potteries in its products, sponsored a comprehensive survey of all buildings in the City surviving from before World War I. This was financed by the Manpower Services Commission as one of their schemes to relieve unemployment. A very detailed record of many of the factories, houses, institutional buildings and other structures was compiled, both as a permanent record of a rapidly diminishing resource and as a means of gaining access to an aspect of the history of the society not available in other sources. The present work, though going far beyond it, draws substantially on the Stoke-on-Trent Historic Buildings Survey in dealing with those buildings that are central to the architectural heritage of the City, the potworks.

It is not fanciful to see in those buildings some characteristics of Potteries' society as it has evolved from its semi-rural origins: its inborn conservatism, its modesty, its esteem for craftsmanship, its tendency to adapt and adjust rather than sweep away with radical innovations, its attention to appearance where it was thought to matter, in the façades, and its almost total indifference to orderliness, planned process and mechanisation, in the actual workplace. It is a society in which the initiative was left to men of moderate means. Those with great power were prepared to exploit its resources to the full: sadly, they put very little back. The Potteries was left to make itself. Almost the only intervention from outside came in the form of the Federation of 1910, which changed little. With a population now of nearly a quarter of a million the Potteries remains what it was, a city with the heart and mind of a village.

Chapter 1

POTTERY MANUFACTURE BEFORE 1700

The Potteries lies on the edge of the Staffordshire moorlands close to the plain of Cheshire. Geologically, the area stands on the North Staffordshire Coalfield, which has outcrops of some thirty coal seams and important layers of ironstone and clay. To the east is the dark grey clay of the Black Band group, interspersed with coal and ironstone seams, while to the west in the upper coal measures are the beds of Etruria Marl.[1] The combination of shallow mineral layers and heavy clay soil dictated that this would never be a prosperous agricultural region. Rather, the close proximity of workable coal, clay and ironstone made possible an industrial future. The importance of these minerals to the development of the area is reflected in the positions of its six towns (Burslem, Fenton, Hanley, Longton, Stoke and Tunstall), which run in a line from north to south along the coalfield (Map 1). All three minerals have been exploited for centuries, surface outcropping making them easily accessible even to those without the technology necessary for deep mining, or the means to afford it. While the coal and iron industries were to become major employers, it was pottery-manufacturing which was to establish itself as the distinctive feature of North Staffordshire and to give the district its name and unique industrial heritage.

The earliest evidence of pottery-making in the area comes from an archaeological excavation of a Roman settlement at Trent Vale.[2] This uncovered traces of a kiln, workshop and sherds of cooking vessels. Other excavations have brought to light evidence that a local pottery industry was in existence by the late thirteenth century. The most significant medieval pottery-making site so far discovered is at Sneyd Green, near Burslem, where two kiln bases and a large quantity of thirteenth-century waste pottery have been found.[3] The archaeological evidence of kilns and ware of the medieval period is complemented, from the fourteenth century, by documentary sources which record the presence of a growing pottery industry. The first reference to potters in the Tunstall Manor Court Rolls is in 1348, recording that one 'William le Potter gives the lord 6d to have licence to make earthen pot'.[4]

Burslem is traditionally held to be the earliest pottery-manufacturing centre in the area, an assertion given weight by the discovery of a number of pottery-waste sites in the area which date from the sixteenth and seventeenth centuries.[5] Certainly, by the end of the seventeenth century, it was Burslem which had gained the reputation for being 'where the greatest pottery made in this county is carried on'.[6] By this period, however, Hanley and Shelton had also become an established centre of pot-making, the Manor Court Rolls for that area frequently recording fines on all those 'who dig pitt or pitts to get claye in the lanes'.[7] From the early seventeenth century there are records of similar fines on potters in the Manor of Longton who were digging clay and leaving the pits unfilled. In both areas the number of entries suggests that this practice was becoming increasingly common.[8] The evidence of the Court Rolls indicates that there was a connection between the pattern of landownership in the district and the development of the pottery-making industry. North Staffordshire was traditionally divided into large estates. The northern area of Burslem and Tunstall was owned mainly by the Sneyd family of Keele. Penkhull, Shelton and part of Hanley belonged to the Duchy of Lancaster, while the northern half of Hanley was an independent manor. The area of Stoke around the church was glebe land owned by the Church of England; the rest belonged to major estates. Fenton also was divided into several large estates, while, to the south, the area of modern Longton was largely under a single manor, later divided into two.

The pattern of landholding varied in each area. Burslem was a community of quite substantial yeomen copyholders, who were able to dig for clay and coal on their land after the Sneyd family had relinquished the mineral rights in 1611. In Hanley and Shelton, the Duchy of Lancaster let its land to copyhold tenants, whilst retaining the mineral rights to the whole area, which it let separately. Alongside these copyholders there developed a settlement founded on the wastes, common land of little value to the Duchy, on which individuals were allowed to erect their

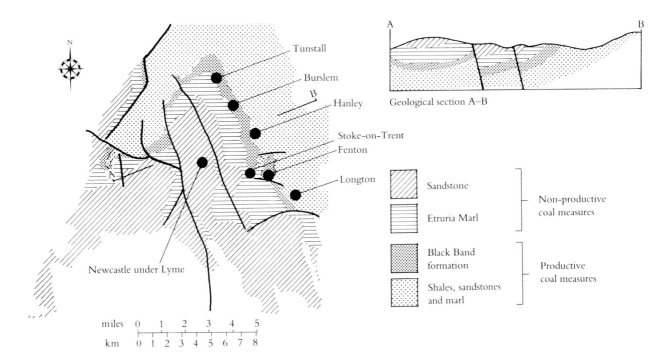

Map 1
The geology of the Staffordshire Potteries

cottages and pottery workhouses. While some copyholders dug clay on their own land and a number of more affluent tenants worked coal mines, the cottagers on the wastes dug for both clay and coal wherever they were able to, the latter in areas where seams came to the surface and mining needed neither expensive equipment nor great effort. Tolerance of the embryonic pottery industry was not unqualified. In 1659 Margaret Griffin was fined for building workhouses and pot ovens on the waste, presumably without permission, and there were the aforementioned fines on other individuals who dug for clay and coal without filling in the pits afterwards. Nevertheless, the local inhabitants persisted, and it was on such waste land throughout the district that much of the industry came to be based.

The Staffordshire potters of the seventeenth century came from a wide range of social and economic backgrounds, from wealthy yeomen down to cottagers scraping a living at, or near, subsistence level. One feature characteristic of potters both rich and poor is that they, like so many engaged in craft industries at that time,

combined a manufacturing activity with the cultivation of land. The evidence of wills and probate inventories provides valuable information about the nature of the industry at this stage in its development, particularly the extent to which it was combined with agriculture in a dual economy. The wealth of individual potters at the time of death varied considerably, a Burslem yeoman, Richard Daniels, leaving an estate worth £421 in 1687, while William Simpson of Hanley, who died in 1707, left only £11 6s 8d.[9] In many cases the proportion of a potter's assets tied up in agriculture was far greater than that in his pottery-manufacturing business. For example, when Thomas Dakin, a Shelton potter, died in 1680 leaving an estate valued at £31 1s 0d, £20 of this was in animals and hay, and only £3 1s 0d in pottery-making equipment, stock and raw materials. Of the latter sum, £1 4s 0d was for 'beating boards, clay, and all other materials belonging to his trade of potting', and 'potts ready made'.[10]

The fact that the agricultural assets of individual potters were usually greater than those related to pottery-manufacturing does not necessarily mean that the former occupation was any more important in financial terms. In this period pottery manufacture was still a domestic, craft industry, requiring only a relatively modest outlay for the equipment and raw materials needed to set up in business. For this reason comparisons between the proportions of capital tied up in industry and in agriculture are not very meaningful, giving no real clue to the relative importance of the two sources of income.[11]

The buildings in which the pottery was made varied according to the means of the individual potter. Pottery-making was a domestic industry, usually involving the whole of a potter's family; and while it could not easily take place within the living quarters of the potter, as with some crafts, it could be carried out in buildings alongside his dwelling. Potters of yeoman status were able to establish their potworks as a part of their farmsteads, using existing agricultural buildings or erecting purpose-built structures, these including a kiln in the yard in which to fire their pots.

Unfortunately, no seventeenth-century potworks survive. Instead, illustrations and documentary sources provide the only evidence. These do, however, allow the reasonably accurate reconstructions of such works. The pictures which

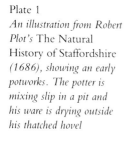

Plate 1
An illustration from Robert Plot's The Natural History of Staffordshire *(1686), showing an early potworks. The potter is mixing slip in a pit and his ware is drying outside his thatched hovel*

emerge are of ranges of single or two-storeyed buildings, often thatched, that include the potter's dwelling, his workhouse and kiln (Plate 1). In some cases, workhouse and kiln were detached from the dwelling, while larger manufacturers might have two or more workhouses. The best surviving illustration of a potworks of the latter kind is provided by a nineteenth-century illustration of the Churchyard Works in Burslem, belonging to the great-great-grandfather of Josiah Wedgwood, and dating from the mid seventeenth century. The illustration shows a substantial two-storeyed, thatched house with the works, including the pot ovens, in the yard behind (Plate 2). By this time the kilns had become semi-permanent structures of stone or brick. Robert Plot on his visit to Staffordshire in 1677 described them as being 'ordinarily about eight feet high, and six feet wide, of a round copped form, where [the pots] are placed one upon another from the bottom to the top'.[12]

The kilns described are of similar shape, but without the enclosing bottle-shaped chimney or 'hovel' and much smaller than the kilns of the nineteenth and twentieth centuries. Two factors combined to determine the form of the potworks at this stage in the industry's development. The first was the fact that pottery-making was carried

out on a relatively small scale and did not, therefore, need large buildings to accommodate it; the second that the types and range of ware being produced, and the methods of production, were relatively limited. The majority of potters worked on their own, or with the assistance of their families, making mainly coarse domestic pottery such as butter pots, milk pans and storage vessels. Many appear to have specialised in one particular line rather than producing a wider range. The materials and methods used were few. The pots were either thrown on the wheel or press-moulded out of ordinary local clay. They were then coated and decorated with coloured slips made from the clay, and brushed with a simple lead glaze. After a single firing in the oven they were taken for sale by the pedlars or cratesmen.

The potter's equipment was confined to implements for preparing the clay and materials – a throwing wheel and slip and glaze buckets. In 1676, for example, Raph Simpson died owning 'boards, shovells, paddles, potwheels, mortar and pestill'.[13] The structural requirements of the early potter were obviously limited. He needed space for his wheel and an area for decorating. External space was as important to him as internal, for he left his clay outside to be weathered, usually blunged or mixed his slip in outside pits, and spread out his pots in the open air to dry. The area around the buildings was used as an extension of the workshop: for example, in 1703 one potter in Hanley kept 'in the lane by the workhouse: lyme and soyle mixt, clay, glass bottles, table baskets and odd things'.[14] The larger potter would have had more than one workhouse, but given the simplicity of production there was no need for separate rooms for different parts of the process, or different types of ware.

A detailed study of Burslem wills and inventories from 1660 to 1732 shows that while the workhouse and pot house were present at the beginning of the period, the only other references to additional buildings or rooms to appear before the end of the seventeenth century were for a smoke house in which unfired ware was dried, in 1669, and a warehouse, in 1679.[15]

The simple structures and small rural communities which accommodated the craft of pot-making should not, however, lead to underestimation of its importance at this early stage in its evolution. Over the generations a solid base of industry had been laid and experience accumulated which made the area receptive to new developments and ready to enter the industrial age.

Plate 2
The Churchyard Works, Burslem, c1659: a more substantial and sophisticated homestead and potworks than the simple structure shown in the previous illustration

Chapter 2

THE DEVELOPMENT OF POTWORKS DURING THE EIGHTEENTH CENTURY

During the first part of the eighteenth century potworks began to proliferate around the centres of settlement (Plate 3), although they were still, for the most part, relatively small concerns. A list later compiled by Josiah Wedgwood estimated that in the years between 1710 and 1715, the average works employed no more than six men and four boys.[1] One early Victorian writer described a typical potworks of the first half of the eighteenth century as comprising:

One hovel, with thatched sheds, as workshops, attached for the Thrower, Presser, Handler (Stouker), and other operatives, perhaps from five to eight in number at a single work; and a drying shed...a tank for preparing the diluted clay...with a smoke house, as it was termed, for drying the green ware more expeditiously...[2]

Many potters continued to work from rented cottages on the wastes. One such was the Hanley potter, John Simpson, who in 1740 occupied 'two workhouses called the Upper Workhouse and a Barn standing on the said wasteland...And also 12 yards in length and 26 yards in breadth of waste land lying at the end of the garden betwixt the said Upper Workhouse and the Barn'.[3] In addition to this, he was allowed 'to make use of 16 yards in length of the waste ground lying before the said Upper Workhouse for drying his pots and earthenware thereon'.[4]

It was by no means uncommon in this period for houses to be converted into potworks. In 1750, for example, Humphrey Palmer was leasing a works in Snape Marsh which included 'two pot ovens and hovells, a stove, a smoak house, a packing house and slip kilns', these having been converted from a house accommodating seven inhabitants.[5] Conversely, Edward Glass of Hanley sold his family's house and barns together with 'all that other piece of building there which was formerly used by [his father]...as a workehouse to make pots in but is now converted into dwellings'.[6]

Although still a craft industry in which men of small means predominated, a number of concerns were already becoming increasingly capital-intensive. One such was the firm of Hill and Fenton, which in 1720 employed ten men at its works in Shelton.[7] By the following year the same firm owned a purpose-built workshop three storeys high, a building considered of sufficient interest to be mentioned specifically in a legal document.[8]

CHANGING DEMAND AND TECHNICAL INNOVATIONS

The gradually increasing scale and specialisation of the industry as it moved from its domestic to factory phase was to have a considerable impact on the economy of the area. One of the first effects was a decline in the traditional practice of dual occupation, potters abandoning farming in order to concentrate exclusively on manufacturing. However, the single most important factor in the development of the industry in the first half of the eighteenth century was the emergence of a completely new branch, the manufacture of fine tableware. Initially, the demand for this ware, created by the growing popularity of tea and coffee drinking, was met by imports from the Far East. It was not long, though, before English potters, eager to profit by the new fashion, began to experiment with imitations of the Chinese ware.

The first copies were made in London, Bristol and Liverpool, the places where the original ware was first seen. As imports increased in the 1720s and spread through the country, so the Staffordshire potters, too, became familiar with the new ware and began to attempt to make their own copies of it.[9] The major problem which faced them was that the locally dug clays were not suitable for manufacturing the fine ware. Some potters, including the Elers Brothers of Bradwell, had already begun to produce the new ware from laboriously refined local clays around the turn of the century. What the potters really needed, though, was a dense white material which would make delicate pottery and show off colour decoration. It is said that it was the Shelton potter,

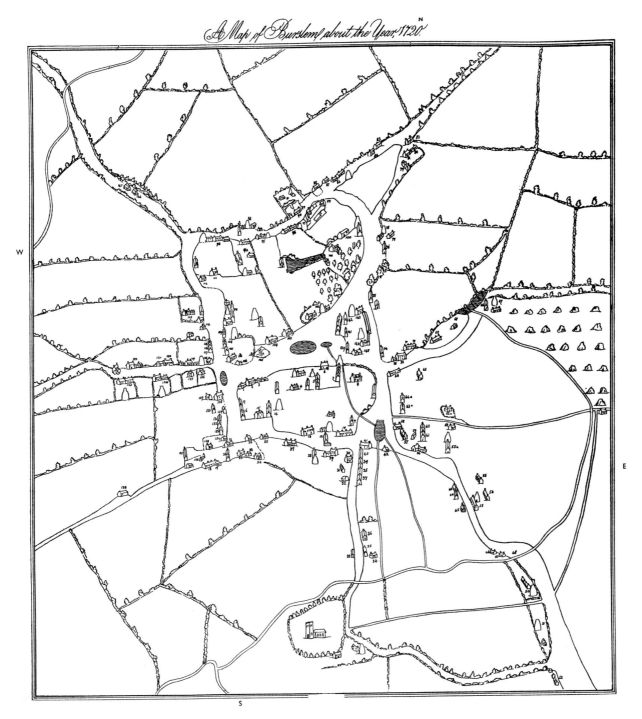

A Map of Burslem, about the Year 1720.

Thomas Astbury, who, in 1720, first discovered that ground flint could be used both to harden and to whiten clay. Around the same date it was found that ball clay produced the type of fine white body required. The problems with these solutions were that neither flint nor ball clay was native to the area, the former being found in chalk formations, the latter only in Devon. Both materials, therefore, would have to be transported considerable distances, a necessity which was to make the improvement of communications of growing importance to the industry as the century progressed.

Despite the problems created by poor communications, quantities of flint and ball clay were brought into the area, often by larger pottery manufacturers. As well as importing the materials for their own use, some appear to have acted as merchants – selling a proportion on to smaller potters who would otherwise have been unable to

Plate 3
An early nineteenth-century copy of a map of Burslem c1720, showing potworks scattered around the ancient settlement

secure a supply. Not surprisingly, many potters appear to have been keen to turn their hands to making cream tableware, as well as the traditional local red ware.

The processes involved in the production of the new ware were more complex than those of the local red ware. This growing sophistication required corresponding changes in the internal arrangements of the potworks, the new ware requiring a greater number of separate rooms than had previously been necessary. Further subdivision of a works was required if it continued to produce red as well as cream ware.

It was important that the manufacturing processes of the two wares were kept separate in order to avoid the contamination of the raw materials. In addition, the introduction of plaster moulds, around 1740, necessitated not only the provision of an area for mould-making and drying, but also added a further method of throwing and pressing pots.

The first known reference to a throwing room occurs in 1731[10] and to a slip house in 1732.[11] The new forms of fine domestic ware also needed turning (trimming on a lathe), as a result of which turning houses also became features of potworks from at least this decade. The pots had to be given handles and spouts, which were attached in handling rooms, and the first references to these rooms also begin to appear in the 1730s.[12]

Further, there were new glazes and methods of decoration which also demanded separate areas; while the warehouse now became an important part of the works, being used for sorting, packing and displaying as well as storage prior to dispatch.

Divisions continued into the firing processes of the potworks. Saggars (containers made of a coarse clay) had long been used on a small scale in the traditional potteries. The glazed pots were placed inside the saggars, which could then be stacked inside the kiln for firing. In the eighteenth century, saggars became much more important, because the individual pieces of the new ware needed to be separated during firing to prevent the glazes sticking, and also to be protected from damage by the flames and fumes of the fuel. Hence the saggar-making shop, and the placing-area near the kiln where the pots were put inside the saggars, became common to all potworks.

The introduction of new wares and increased overall production had implications for both the size and the number of ovens required. Previously the pots had been fired only once; but the fineness and intricacy of the new shapes and their un-suitability for powdered glazing now meant that an initial, 'biscuit' firing was necessary, followed by dipping in liquid glaze, and a second 'glost'

firing. The potter could either alternate these firings, or build a second oven for the purpose. In most cases it is impossible to determine whether the presence of two kilns at a potworks indicates separate biscuit and glost ovens, but excavations at the Pomona Works in Newcastle under Lyme have shown this to be so, with the two kilns dating from around 1724.[13] Similarly, one of the kilns at the 1750s' Longton Hall site appears to have been used solely for biscuit firing.[14] The number and type of ovens were also affected by the introduction, by 1750, of enamel painting. This involved only a percentage of the ware, but required its own low-temperature firing after the glost firing.

EXPANSION OF THE POTWORKS

As a result of increased production, potters began to expand their works, and, as their wealth grew, to build substantial houses for themselves. One of the first to put up a purpose-built works was Thomas Whieldon. The potworks in Fenton, which he had occupied as a tenant, was later described as 'a small range of low buildings, all thatched'.[15] By the time he bought the property, in 1748, this range had been replaced, or at least extended, by the building of a new potworks comprising 'pot ovens, houses, buildings, warehouses, workhouses, hovels, stores, throwing houses and other conveniences...lately built and made for the carrying on the trade of a potter'.[16]

Whieldon was one of the earliest potters, possibly even the first, to create what was effectively a pottery estate. In 1749, the year after he bought his works, he purchased the estate at which it was situated, along with which he acquired Fenton Hall. He did not, however, live in the Hall, but instead built himself another mansion nearby, The Grove, and assumed the role of landed gentleman. Moreover, by 1750 he owned several groups of cottages, at least some of which were occupied by workmen in his employment.[17]

By the 1760s a number of other substantial pottery-manufacturing concerns had developed in the area. An inventory drawn up in 1761 reveals that John Baddeley held an extensive works in Shelton (on the site of Mason's Ironstone factory in Broad Street). This comprised a saggar-making house, two separate saggar houses, a china slip house and second slip house, three throwing houses, a handling house, two drying rooms, a biscuit oven and a glost oven, a black ware dipping house, a china dipping room and a red and black warehouse.[18] There was also an accounting house, a further indication of the size

Plate 4
The Big House, Burslem, built for John and Thomas Wedgwood in 1751

of the business. Documentary sources point to the existence of other similarly large businesses by this date. William Banks, for example, insured his potworks in Stoke (subsequently those of Josiah Spode) for £486; his policy entry listing a range of workhouses is similar to Baddeley's.[19]

Like Whieldon, these wealthier potters aspired to increasingly large and impressive houses. The Baddeley family, for instance, lived in the White House, one of the principal houses in the district. Situated in front of their works, this had two parlours, three bedrooms, kitchen, cellar, wash-house, brewhouse, 'little room', lobby and two garretts.[20] Another large manufacturer's house, the Big House in Burslem, which was built for John and Thomas Wedgwood in 1751, is a symmetrical three-storeyed brick building with a projecting central bay surmounted by a pediment (Plates 4 and 5).

WINDMILLS AND WATER MILLS

The introduction of the new wares not only changed the nature of the industry, but also led to the establishment of separate, though related, activities. One of these was flint-grinding.

Initially, the process of finely grinding flint prior to its mixing with the clay was done by hand. This was possible when only small quantities were required, but impractical when demand grew.

Plate 5
Staircase of the Big House, Burslem

Horse-powered flint mills were also used, and by the middle of the century some potters had adapted or erected windmills for wet-grinding their raw materials. Around 1750 the canal engineer and millwright James Brindley rented a millwright's shop from Thomas and John Wedgwood and built a mill for them on high ground overlooking Burslem called 'Jenkins'. It is said to have been a four-sailed tower mill, built for wet-grinding flint. There was a circular grinding pan housed in the base of the mill. The wind shaft drove a vertical shaft which rotated sweep arms around the pan, and these pushed around large blocks of stone which crushed the flint and water mix to a fine slurry.[21]

The windmill was a valuable source of power but a limited one, dependent on an appropriate site and capable of only a moderate work load. An alternative was the water mill, which also became an adjunct to the pottery industry. A number of water mills were adapted from corn mills, such as Gomm's Mill, bought by John Peate in Lane Delph in 1732, and the old machine mill at Little Chell, used for potting from 1746.[22] Around this date Thomas Whieldon was operating his own water mill at Fenton, later to be converted to steam by Robert Hamilton.[23] While mills existed, they were few in relation to the number of potworks, and just as corn mills were open for public use, so these mills supplied all the local potters with ground flint. Some of the large potters may have been influenced in the location

of their works by the presence of water for erecting a water mill, but suitable locations in the Potteries were few and far between, as a result of which many mills came to be sited some distance away, mainly along the Churnet and Moddershall Valleys. In all, thirty-five flint and colour-grinding mills were eventually to be established along these watercourses, thus supplying a significant proportion of the industry's requirements. Two water-powered mills have been restored and opened to the public, the Mostylee Mill near Moddershall, built as a corn mill in 1716 and converted to flint-grinding in 1756, and the South Mill at Cheddleton (Plate 6), built some time after 1783.[24]

The flint was brought into the area by several routes, one being from Liverpool via the River Weaver to Winsford; another from Hull via the River Trent to Willington. From these terminal points the flint had to be carried by packhorse to the mills and from them to the potworks. It was a slow and expensive method of transport, unable to cope with movement of goods in bulk. The difficulties and frustrations of the system were voiced by the Shelton potter, John Baddeley, who operated four mills at various times between 1758 and 1763, at least two of which were in the Moddershall Valley. Baddeley and his partner in one of the mills petitioned the Trustees of the Newcastle and Uttoxeter Turnpike Road, complaining against the high tolls they had to pay for the regular, vital journeys.[25]

Plate 6
Cheddleton Flint Mill, converted from a corn-grinding mill in the late eighteenth century

IMPROVEMENTS IN COMMUNICATIONS

By the beginning of the second half of the century, the area's poor communications were threatening to hinder the continued expansion of the industry, a fact which the potters fully recognised. In 1733 the River Weaver was canalised and the road through Newcastle under Lyme turnpiked, improvements which were of some benefit to the industry, but only a small part of the solution. It was not until the 1750s that the situation began to improve to any significant degree. One of the first steps was provision of a number of turnpike roads. These roads, built largely through the initiative of the major potters of the district, broke the monopoly of the neighbouring borough of Newcastle. In 1759, the road from Uttoxeter through Longton and Stoke was turnpiked, with a secondary road up to Hanley. In 1763, the roads from Newcastle to Leek and Church Lawton were also turnpiked, and in 1765 the main road from Newcastle to Burslem. The major step forward, however, was the building of the Trent and Mersey Canal, begun in 1766. As well as the main canal, vital to the communications between the Potteries and other parts of the country and, indeed, the world, there were to be a number of small branch canals in the Potteries, later acting as feeders to the Grand Trunk System. The first of these was the Caldon Canal from Shelton to Leek and Froghall (1773), which was followed by the Froghall Canal from Froghall to Uttoxeter (1797), the Longport to Burslem branch of the Grand Trunk (1797) and the Newcastle Canal from Stoke to Newcastle (1795).[26]

These canals varied in their usage, but were generally built to serve potworks (Plate 7) and collieries, and to provide links to outlying flint mills. Together, the new road and canal networks were to open up the markets of the world to the North Staffordshire pottery industry (Maps 2 and 3).

What, then, were the implications of these improvements in the transport system for the siting of potworks? Proximity to workable deposits of clay was no longer so important since much of the clay used, with the exception of locally quarried saggar marl, was brought in from the south of the country. In theory it would seem that in a period in which imported clay was becoming predominant, and the markets for Staffordshire wares were expanding, canal-side locations for potworks would be the most attractive. If importing the clay and transporting the finished goods had been the priorities, this would almost certainly have been the case, but in fact they were not, and relatively few potters built

Plate 7
Barges tied up at The Eastwood Pottery, Hanley, 1952. The canal is still used to transport ware to different parts of the site by barge

Map 2
The location of the Staffordshire Potteries

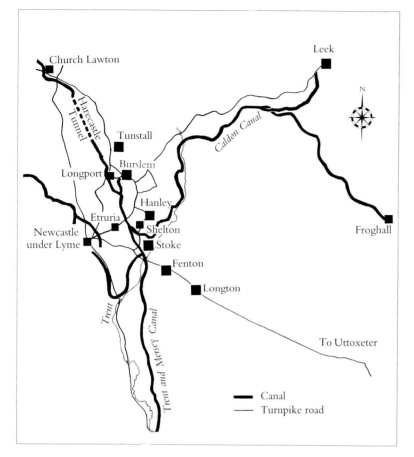

Map 3
The communications network established in the Staffordshire Potteries by the end of the eighteenth century

works alongside canals. One reason for this appears to have been that any access to coal was more significant than access to clay, since for every ton of clay used, five to ten tons of coal were required.[27] This coal was transported mainly by road, making sites close to good turnpiked roads, particularly if also near canals, the most attractive places to build potworks. It has been found that towards the end of the century the areas developing fastest were those along the Burslem to Hanley ridge, the traditional seat of the industry, and on the Newcastle to Derby turnpike where it crossed coal outcrops at Fenton and Longton. At these places, suitable coal could be fetched easily by horse and cart and, later in the century, horse-drawn tramways.

Another consideration was that it was often more expensive to build works alongside the canal since, as these skirted the established centres of population, so the manufacturers not only had to build themselves new potworks, but also houses for themselves and their workers. This was certainly the case with Josiah Wedgwood, who in 1767 paid £3,000 for the 350-acre (142-ha) Ridge House Estate on which he built his works and houses for himself, his partner Thomas Bentley and for a proportion of his workforce.

Foremost among the promoters of the Trent and Mersey Canal, Wedgwood lobbied equally hard to ensure that the line of the canal came as close as possible to his new estate. In 1767 he complained of the overseer, Hugh Henshall: 'I could not prevail upon the inflexible vandal to give me one line of grace'.[28] He did not give up, however, and in the following year faced criticism from fellow potters over a route he proposed which would take the canal alongside his factory, writing that:

> *Some of my good neighbours have taken it into their heads to think that I shall have too pleasant and valuable an situation by the side of the canal, as is planned and executed through my estate. This has raised a little envy in their breasts, and as they are Proprietors, they have represented to the Committee that the Canal ought to be made along the meadows, as that is the shortest and most natural course.*[29]

Wedgwood prevailed in the end, the line chosen for the canal being perfect for his new works. That he should have won the day is not surprising, given the crucial role that he had played in the scheme from the outset. It was in recognition of his part in the venture that he was invited to cut the first turf of the workings, the turf being ceremonially barrowed away by the canal's engineer, James Brindley.

A number of others followed Wedgwood's lead in acquiring land for potworks along the line of the proposed navigation. Amongst these was John Brindley, brother of the canal engineer, who erected a works at Longport around 1773 in anticipation of the new canal. This was followed shortly afterwards by two more, built by Edward Bourne and Robert Williamson.[30] Other manufacturers to build close to the canal system were Josiah Spode, Thomas Minton (from 1793) and Thomas Wolfe (from 1781), all served by the Newcastle Canal. More potters were to build alongside the canals in the following century, but only as land became available. Again these tended to be the leading concerns such as the Eastwood and Cauldon Place Works.

LANDOWNERSHIP AND THE POTWORKS

The question of landownership was crucial to the whole development of the pottery industry and of new communities. The accumulation of land by the most prominent potters and their hopes for social status had led them to lead lives consistent with the traditional landed gentry. The houses they built were surrounded by parkland and a rural environment, and while, as manufacturers, they were eager to promote the industry, they had no wish to see industrial development encroaching on their own estates. Such an attitude was witnessed by Aikin in 1795 in his descriptions of some of the estates. Of Newfield, the estate of the potter and landowner Smith Child, he wrote:

> Newfield...is well situated for manufacturing purposes, having plenty of coals in its neighbourhood; but as the place belongs wholly to one individual, Smith Child, Esq., who has a handsome seat there, it is probable that he will not suffer himself to be incommoded by a consequence inevitable where there are a number of manufactories of earthenware together, the nuisance of the smoke and sulphur arising from them. It is therefore supposed that the manufactories will not be speedily increased here.[31]

All the tensions between gentry and trade were as apparent in North Staffordshire as elsewhere in this period, with the irony that there were those who were both 'gentlemen' and potters.

While the gentlemen potters were establishing themselves on the best plots available, and the more modest copyholders built on their own land, the many small potters continued to work where they could. On the whole, the major landowners acted as a negative factor in industrial development, by not releasing land, or by leasing plots in a controlled way so that development would not be detrimental to the estate. A notable example occurred in Longton, where the two large estates of the Stafford and Foley (from 1784 Heathcote) families were involved. Here, the land on which building was allowed was largely waste land, though it must be admitted that to some extent this satisfied the potters, for the stretch of land included the road through to Uttoxeter, and enabled them to build potworks alongside it. The restriction was not so tight in Hanley and Shelton, under the lordship of the Duchy of Lancaster. It was the mineral rights which were of importance and value to the Duchy, not what lay on top of the land, and the growth of the pottery industry was actually encouraged in the area. In the later eighteenth century, Granville Earl Gower, lessee of the mineral rights and waste in Hanley and Shelton, was imposing low rents on his tenants ostensibly to encourage the industry. To have demanded more rent

> would not only have been injurious but the utter Ruin of many who had borrowed to enable them to build depending on their industry to repay it. It would also have greatly destructed the future increase of the manufactory. At present every body who chooses is permitted to build on the Waste on payment of a small acknowledgement to the lessee.[32]

Towards the end of the century, therefore, it was the most prosperous, long-standing potters who began to move further out to build more ambitious potworks. It was they who built along the main roads, and to a lesser extent along the canals, creating new communities and drawing previously rural estates into the expanding urban areas. Meanwhile, the old centres of potting remained, proliferating in small potworks and cottage dwellings. Together, the two formed the basis of nineteenth-century urban development.

THE DEVELOPMENT OF POTTERY ESTATES

The pottery estates of the large manufacturers, of which the Whieldon Estate was an early example, became common in the latter half of the eighteenth century. Few of these estates comprised complete self-contained communities, and neither was it the case that all of the major manufacturers moved out of the centres to establish their domains. Nevertheless, the new communities form an important part of the development of the industry and the six towns. These estates were organised in such a way as to place the manufacturer's house in the prime position, surrounded by parkland and hidden from the view of the factory. Illustrations always show the master's house in the foreground, with the works, if included at all, far in the distance, a reminder of the source of wealth but not prominent enough to detract from the desired impression of the potter's status. Potworks and workers' housing remained together elsewhere on the estate, the former situated advantageously for transport and resources, the latter having convenience for the works as their only consideration. With the growth in the number of employees and the planned organisation of the potworks, the relationship between the manufacturer and workers became a combination of the old rural landlord and tenant and the new industrial master and employee. It amounted to a relationship of control and deference, and was applicable both in the place of work and in all other aspects of local daily life.

Etruria
The first large planned industrial community in the Potteries, and one of the most well known in the country, was Etruria, built by Josiah Wedgwood between 1767 and 1773. Wedgwood started out in the industry at his grandfather's Churchyard Pottery, moved from there to the Ivy

Plate 8
*The Ivy House Works,
probably built in the early
eighteenth century, rented
by Josiah Wedgwood
1759–62. The potter's
house is seen in the
foreground, with a range of
two-storeyed workshops
behind*

House Works, and then to the Brick-House or Bell Works: each reflected the stages in progression of pottery architecture (Plates 8 and 9). Like other leading potters, however, he needed more than existing potworks could offer, and began looking for potential sites.

The site he chose was the Ridge House Estate, between Hanley and Newcastle. The new community to be founded on it was given the name Etruria, as a result of an erroneously held belief that the classical ware which Wedgwood copied there was Etruscan (in fact, the excavated pottery it was based on was not Etruscan but Attic Greek). The potworks itself was erected alongside the turnpike road between Newcastle and Hanley and, as has been seen (p 16), also fronted on to the planned Trent and Mersey Canal. To the north east of the works, Wedgwood built Etruria Hall for himself, near enough to his business but on rising ground, and masked from the works by a plantation. To the east was a farm, while also in the park he built Bank House for his partner Bentley. To the west of the works he laid out a street or 'town' of forty-two terraced houses for his workers which, in contrast to his own house, was situated on low land next to the works between the canal and the Foulea Brook. The first

estimate for the whole building programme was almost £10,000, but the eventual cost is believed to have been far in excess of this sum.[33] Sadly, all that remains of the Etruria Estate today is the Hall; the factory and housing were demolished in the 1960s.

Etruria was not a complete or model industrial village in the nineteenth-century sense, but there were communal bakehouses and probably shops to serve the houses. An inn was built at some stage and in the nineteenth century a school and chapel were added. It may be that Wedgwood conceived it as a community with the range of facilities being provided over time, as in fact happened. In his own lifetime the essentials of the pottery manufactory and housing were in themselves a major undertaking, demanding in money and time. If not truly a model community, Etruria was sufficient an achievement for its acclaim to continue well into the following century.

In designing Etruria, Wedgwood worked closely with his architect, Joseph Pickford, of Derby. Pickford had been introduced to Wedgwood by John Whitehurst, the horologer, also of Derby. Both Wedgwood and Whitehurst were members of the Lunar Circle, an influential

and exclusive network.[34] Another member was Matthew Boulton, whose Soho factory, near Birmingham (built 1764–6), undoubtedly influenced Wedgwood's thinking in planning his new works. Boulton's Palladian factory, designed by William Wyatt II (assisted by Benjamin Wyatt II), was regarded by contemporaries as a marvel of industrial organisation.[35]

Etruria, like Soho, was the product of the collaboration of architect and industrialist. The role of the latter cannot be overstated, for while an architect might be responsible for details of construction and style, the determining of the layout of the works fell, inevitably, to those who knew the industry best, the manufacturers themselves. For example, it was said to be the 'well-known abilities' of the Fenton potter, William Greatbatch, which 'caused him to be consulted, and to form the plan' for Admiral Smith Child's new potworks at Newfield, near Tunstall in 1763.[36]

Wedgwood's original plan for the Etruria Works was to have three groups of buildings, each around its own courtyard, with walled yards between the central group and those on either side, used for the storage of coal, clay and other materials.

A sketch plan of the period (Plate 10) makes it clear that he intended originally to place hovels for the ovens at each corner of the central group and at the inner ends of the blocks to either side, in other words as close as possible to the coal stored in the yards.[37] The rear of the building was to be screened by a plantation of trees.

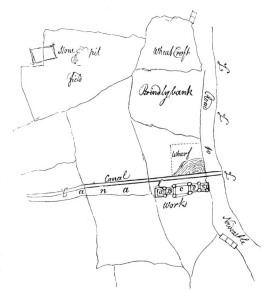

Plate 9
The Brick-House or Bell Works, occupied by Josiah Wedgwood from 1762 to 1773. The works was originally built by John Adams in the mid seventeenth century but is thought to have been rebuilt in the following century. The view shows an enclosed courtyard arrangement, with bottle ovens

Plate 10
Sketch of the Ridge House Estate by Josiah Wedgwood, showing the layout of the Etruria Works as originally envisaged

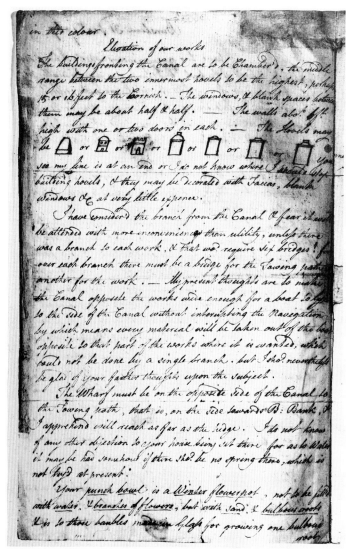

The front elevation of the works, following the example of Boulton's Soho factory, was to be Palladian, the rational architecture of the Age of Reason, and as such the obvious choice for manufacturers of the outlook of Boulton and Wedgwood, who prided themselves on being scientists and men of letters as well as industrialists. This rationalisation notwithstanding, some consideration was given to combining the Palladian style with elements drawn from the then only recently revived Gothick, but Wedgwood was not happy with the idea of combining the two styles, arguing with his partner:

> will not Gothick Battlements to buildings in every other respect in the modern taste be a little heterogenious [sic]? I should be glad to have your thoughts on that point as I do not think my other finish looks so well for the hovels but had given it up on account of its incongruity (pardon this hard word) with the rest of the building.[41]

Interestingly enough, Wedgwood himself had considered giving a Gothick treatment to hovels, as is evident from a letter to Bentley that included sketches of seven ornamental hovels – one with battlements (Plate 11). In the same letter he lightheartedly declared that he did not know when he 'should stop building hovels', which structures might 'be decorated with Facias, blank windows, &c. at a very little expense'.

It is fitting, perhaps, that the only building of the Etruria Works to survive is a circular structure bearing a striking resemblance to one of Wedgwood's sketches (Plate 12). It is not clear

Plate 11
Extract of a letter from Josiah Wedgwood to his partner Bentley, showing his design for hovels

Plate 12
The Round House, Etruria

Wedgwood concerned himself not only with the layout of the works, but also with its outward appearance. Even the details of the treatment of the front elevation were not left to Pickford alone, both Wedgwood and Bentley having their own views on the subject. In a letter to his partner in 1768, Wedgwood wrote: 'The Elevation for the works is very pretty and I wish they were built in the form you have drawn them'.[38] He was worried, though, that the hovels, which were to be placed at the corners of the workshops, would dwarf the front elevation of the building 'which shod. [sic] be capital, down into a diminutive part'.[39] Instead, he felt that what was needed was to reduce the height of the hovels, make the ends of the roofs hipped and put a 'lantern or cupola' over the central block. The latter, he believed, would 'serve both to hang the bell in' and 'to raise the middle part so as to give it the air of principal member of the whole as I think it should have'.[40]

whether the structure, The Round House, was built as a hovel and later converted into an office, or as an office but purposefully given the outward appearance of a hovel. Such a treatment would certainly have been consistent with Wedgwood's whimsical interest in these structures. The roof of the building has a brick dome, concealed beneath a covering of tiles. The entrance facing on to the canal towpath was flanked by a pair of sash windows; the first floor was lit by circular windows.

As built, the Etruria Works were not dissimilar in layout to the original sketches. The only obvious departure is that hovels were not placed at the corners of the central block.

In accordance with Wedgwood's wishes, the front elevation of the central block was designed in such a way as to focus attention on the centre of the façade. This was achieved by giving it a projecting central bay with pediment over; above this was an imposing cupola, in which was hung the bell brought from his Brick-House Works.

The effect was further enhanced by the fenestration of the central bay, the first floor having a Diocletian window, the second a large tripartite one. The front elevation of Etruria, like so many textile mills of the second half of the century, owed much to the more restrained country house Palladianism of the period, the area of work in which its architect, Pickford, was most at home (Plate 13).

The façade of Etruria was very influential, variations on it being the most common works frontage in the Potteries for more than a hundred years. One of the few surviving street elevations for a potworks of this period is that of William Adams's Greengates Pottery in Tunstall. This works, dating from the 1780s, has now partly subsided and is hidden from the road by a wall and a more recent building. An early nineteenth-century print, however, shows the works as originally built, depicting a central block of nine bays in length and three storeys in height, flanked

Plate 13
A view of the Etruria Works and the Trent and Mersey Canal, taken in 1898 by an employee at the works

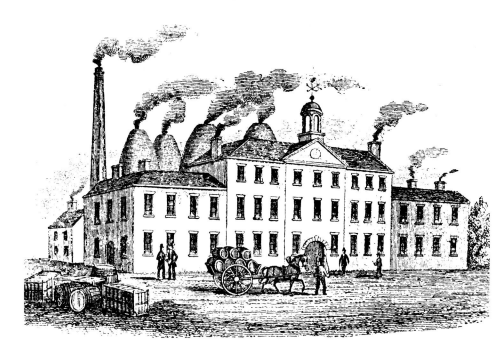

Plate 14
An eighteenth-century illustration of the Greengates Pottery

Plate 15
Greengates Pottery today

by a pair of wings of four bays and two storeys. The three central bays of the main block project and are surmounted by a pediment. Like Etruria, there is a tall cupola in which hung the works bell (Plates 14 and 15).

Other potworks

Not all potters followed Wedgwood in adopting an exclusively Palladian style. The most important exception to the rule was Enoch Wood, whose Fountain Place Works of 1789, in Burslem, was the curious mixture of Palladian and Gothick elements which Wedgwood had wished to avoid twenty years before. The main entrance block to this works is, unfortunately, all that now survives. The corner entrance bay (Plate 16) had a basket-arched opening with Venetian and tripartite windows over, the whole surmounted by a pediment and cupola. Elsewhere in the works, though, it was the Gothick influence that was most pronounced. A pair of early nineteenth-century prints shows the works with a crenellated boundary wall and a wide gateway flanked by crenellated towers. Some of the hovels even have the crenellated tops toyed with by Wedgwood himself (Plates 17 and 18).

SUBDIVISION AND ORGANISATION OF THE POTWORKS

The separation of pottery-making processes
As individual manufacturers produced wider ranges of wares so the practice of physically subdividing the works into more discrete areas of activity continued. Even a potter of apparently

Plate 16
Corner entrance (now blocked) to the former Enoch Wood and Sons Fountain Place Works, Burslem

only average output, such as William Greatbatch of Fenton, was producing cream ware, salt-glazed stoneware, basalt, cane and red ware, using throwing, press-moulding and slip-casting methods, and enamelling, transfer-printing and hand-painting for decoration.[42] Similarly, in Lane

Plate 17
East view of Enoch Wood's Fountain Place Works, Burslem (illustration c1843)

Plate 18
West view of Enoch Wood's Fountain Place Works, Burslem (illustration c1843)

Plate 19
A courtyard at Etruria Works, photographed in the mid 1930s

End in the 1760s, John Turner was said to have 'manufactured every kind of pottery then in demand, and also introduced some others not previously known'.[43]

Etruria was no exception to this trend towards the greater subdivision of potworks. In designing the factory, Wedgwood did not create a single potworks, but a row of three traditional courtyard works (Plate 19), one for the manufacture of 'ornamental work', one for 'plates and dishes' and a third for 'every other sort of useful ware'.[44] In this important respect his approach differed little from what had gone before. Where Etruria did make a break with the past was in terms of the scale of its operation and in its highly organised structure. It was carefully designed for the large-scale and efficient manufacture of a wide range of wares, utilising a variety of clay bodies and a number of different decorative treatments.

At the front of the factory were two long ranges, the northernmost, immediately alongside the canal, comprising warehouses and packing houses, the other slightly set back and consisting

partly of offices. A small opening at the south end of this range appears to have been the only entrance to the works. Adjoining this was a row of six dwellings. The first of these was the porter's lodge with bay window, overlooking the entry and enabling supervision of all movement to and fro. The other buildings were possibly built for workers such as firemen, whose lengthy shifts in tending the ovens required long periods of attendance on site.

Behind this front row of buildings the works was divided into compartments. When production was transferred from the Brick-House Works to Etruria in 1773, it was separated into the ornamental and the useful. To the rear of the warehouses at the north of the site was the ornamental works, with a separate square for the black basalt ware so that it did not contaminate the white clays. In the centre and south courts were the useful works where earthenware pottery was made, divided into particular aspects of production, while at the back of the site was the mill block. An assortment of craft workshops, used for making barrels and crates for example, was on hand.

It should perhaps be noted at this point that by the later part of the eighteenth century the larger manufacturers not only had their ordinary storage warehouses on the potwork site but were also taking on warehouses with showroom facilities in London in order to increase opportunities for sale and to extend the market. In some cases these were run by agents, in others by the potters themselves. A warehouse for the Longton Hall Company was set up in around 1758, and Wedgwood had a pattern room in Charles Street, Grosvenor Square, from 1765. In 1768 he managed to find a large warehouse in St Martin's Lane, a corner house 60 feet long (18 m) in 'the best situation in all London'.[45]

Illustrations, photographs and accounts of Etruria give information otherwise lost to us. The general picture is one of cobbled courtyards surrounded by tightly knit two and three-storeyed buildings, deftly built against the rounded structures of hovels, and with workshops served by external brick and stone staircases. A description of 1920 mentions a number of specific details, such as the semicircular alcoves set into outside walls, which held taps from which water could be carried in buckets.[46] It shows the solid wooden doors with wooden latches and bolts, and the plain small-paned windows to the workshops. There was also the whole oak tree trunk, now at the Wedgwood Museum at Barlaston, which on the first floor formed a block on which moulds were made. The trunk passed through this floor, standing as a column in the workshop below, and had its foundations in the earth. This ingenious arrangement meant that the stress caused by constant hammering on the block did not vibrate the building but was directed through to the earth itself, which also served to deaden the noise.

Though working conditions at Etruria were determined largely by the needs of production and the benefit of the pottery, Wedgwood did display a degree of concern for the workforce that many other manufacturers may not have shared. When examined in front of a Select Committee in 1816, Josiah Wedgwood II claimed that his work people were not crowded together but had ample space. Asked if the rooms were heated, he replied: 'some of the rooms have rooms heated by stoves contiguous to them, for the purpose of drying the ware when placed in a wet space upon the moulds; those drying rooms are necessarily open into the rooms somewhat considerably'. The works as a whole was heated by stove pots and fireplaces. The rooms were not closed: 'the doors are generally open, and there are casements in the windows, which the work people may open at their pleasure, as the temperature is of no importance in the process of the manufacture'.[47] He did not say if he would have allowed such freedom if the temperature *had* been of significance for the ware!

Wedgwood's attention to cleanliness, health and hygiene was far ahead of his time. As a precaution against lead poisoning, dipping rooms were to be cleaned out with a mop, never brushed; a pail of water, soap and brush were always to be at hand; no one was to eat in the dipping room, and those working there wore over-smocks which were to be removed on leaving the room.[48] These regulations came from Wedgwood himself, not from government specifications or guidelines, which did not yet exist. Such provisions were rare, and only came to be enforced by official legislation a century later.

Less is known of other major works erected before the end of the century, but they appear to have conformed to the Etruria pattern by being large industrial concerns broken up into different areas. William Adams of Greengates soon outgrew the works there, but, rather than erecting a separate works beside it, took on a further potworks at Newfield, then using Greengates as an 'ornamental' works in the same way that Wedgwood had divided his production at Etruria.[49] The large new potworks built by Thomas Wolfe in Stoke was of single triangular courtyard plan to fit his site, and divided into many small workshops. It was later split into two parts, and a further works built on the other side of the road.[50] The Enoch Wood Pottery at Fountain Place most clearly exemplifies the large potworks and its small divisions. From the outside it appeared a fine, monumental industrial complex, and was said to have 'such a judicious arrangement that it preserves all the appearance of a most extensive laboratory and the machinery of an Experimentalist'.[51] A series of early nineteenth-century illustrations shows a quite humble set of potworks, however, with a mass of small individual workshops within the grand external shell.[52]

The segregation of the workforce

In these large new manufactories, the division and organisation in the structures became equally apparent with regard to the segregation of the pottery workers. In the small works there was still a degree of versatility and familiarity with all parts of the potworks and of the craft. As Simeon Shaw was to write in 1829: 'to be really useful to the master and secure sufficient employment, a good workman could throw, turn and stack'. In the big new works, however, where production was higher and often more diversified, the labour force was more specialised: each person was trained in a particular skill and stayed within that department. The most obvious benefit to this was that it allowed thorough training and very considerable skills in each area, as well as being more economical in time and movement: 'the dexterity and quickness consequent on separate persons confining themselves solely to one branch of the Art, with the time saved in the change of implements and articles, instead of retarding it greatly promoted the manufacture by increasing its excellence and elegance'.[53]

Segregation had two other important advantages. It allowed a form of control and discipline, made necessary by the loss of trust and intimacy of the small-scale family works, and of the direct relationship between master potter and employees. As the works became larger, over-lookers took on an intermediary position between the two, and an element of their supervisory role became visible architecturally. The small, separate workshops catered for manageable groups, and the use of external staircases not only allowed all movement to be seen, but even further reduced the degree of communication between work-shops. The other advantage was to preserve secrets of the trade. The matter of guarding discoveries, new recipes and techniques was important to potters in this stage of development: a possibly apocryphal but nevertheless instructive tale has been passed down of the jealousy of the Elers brothers of Bradwell in the 1690s over their manufacturing processes which led them to employ idiots in order to preserve the secrets, each person being locked in his place of work and examined before leaving at night.[54]

At Etruria Wedgwood insisted on keeping each workshop separate, 'which I have much set my heart on', despite the complexities which this entailed in a large potworks.[55] The full effect of the arrangement can be seen from a contemporary breakdown of the different workers at the manufactory, which produces an overwhelming list of categories. In the coloured ware section alone were painters, grinders, printers, liners, borderers, burnishers and scourers, while the jasper department had ornamenters, turners, slip-makers, grinders, scourers and mould-makers. In black ware were turners, throwers, handlers, seal-makers, mould-makers and slip-makers; and in all were modellers, firemen, overlookers, porters and packers. Other employees in the works included saggar-makers, lathe turners, spout-makers, wedgers, engravers, polishers, dressers, sorters, dippers, brushers, stirrers, placers and coopers.[56]

The organisation and skills, and the control and maintenance of trade secrets, which lay behind this segregation of workshops and workers are all documented in Wedgwood's corres-pondence with his partner Bentley. With more reason than many, Wedgwood was particularly concerned about workers leaving with his secrets, and was prepared to arrange his works in order to prevent their learning anything of the whole manufacturing process. A letter to Bentley in 1769 makes this clear, and also refers to the use of outside steps to workshops as a means of achieving isolation:

These new hands should if possible be kept by themselves till we are better acquainted with them, otherwise they may do us a great deal of mischief if we should be obliged to part with them soon. I have had some thoughts of building steps to the outside of some of the chambers for that purpose. What think you of it? We cannot avoid taking in strangers and shall be obliged sometimes to part with them again, we should therefore prevent as much as possible their taking any part of our business along with them. Every class should if possible be kept by themselves and have no connection with any others.[57]

Wedgwood continued the practice he had begun at the Bell Works of having a bell to summon his employees to work. They had to report in at the porter's lodge, at the works entrance near to their homes. There were fines for 'any workman scaling the walls of the gates', and

for 'any workmen foreseeing their way through the lodge after the time allowed by the master'.[58] Once within the works, they spent the day in their own workshop in an enclosed courtyard. It is clear that by the later years of the eighteenth century there was a well-defined relationship of control and subservience between the pottery manufacturer and his employees.

Equipment and its implications for potworks' design

Thus two important considerations in the planning of the later eighteenth-century potworks were the provision and arrangement of multiple workshops for the different processes in pot-making, and the corresponding division of the workforce. A third factor was the needs of the equipment used in the industry by this stage. The main point to make is that pottery-making was still largely a hand-craft industry, operated by human power. The 'making' shops, in which the pots were turned, accommodated hand-operated wheels, the actual throwing wheel being worked by a rope pulley leading to a second, vertical wheel turned by an assistant.[59] The other methods of pot-making, slip-casting and press-moulding were done by hand, as were the decorating processes. By the middle of the century the lathe was being used to trim the pots, again powered by an assistant to the turner. In this respect the main concessions necessary to the design of the workshops would have been to provide appropriate space for the individual pieces of equipment and to give consideration to their weight and usage. It is known, for example, that Wedgwood decided 'a ground floor is much better for lathes than a chamber story, the latter are so apt to shake with the motion of the lathe'.[60]

Steam-powered mills

While the structural requirements in the 'making' part of the potworks were basic and sometimes subtle ones, it was the demands of the clay preparation area which most affected building design in the large new works. It has already been seen (pp 13–14) that the powered mill became a dominant part of the potwork complex. As the quality of ware relied on the careful control of clay bodies and glazes, it was obviously advantageous for the potter to have his own mill (if he could afford it) and to find the most efficient source of power for it.

Windmills continued to be used in the industry: Enoch Wood, for example, is known to have erected one at his Fountain Place Works in the 1780s for 'raising water, mixing clay and grinding glazes and colours'.[61] Wedgwood erected a six-sailed tower mill at Etruria soon after the completion of the works.[62] In addition to this, his friend, and colleague in the Lunar Circle, Erasmus Darwin, also designed a horizontal windmill for him, well-documented in correspondence between the two. In an undated letter written between late 1767 and early 1768 Darwin wrote of his intended windmill:

I think it is peculiarly adopted to your kind of Business, where the motion is slow and horizontal. If the mixture of clay or flint and water should grow stiff by the wind ceasing, I think it may be so contrived with ease as to be put into motion again gradually, not suddenly…The advantages are,

1. Its power may be extended much further than the common windmill.

2. It has fewer moving parts.

3. In your Business no Tooth and Pinion-work will be necessary. Plain Countries are preferable to hilly ones for windmills because the wind acquires eddies in the latter.[63]

Having seen a model of the windmill, Wedgwood described it as 'a very ingenious invention'[64] which he hoped would answer his expectations, but Darwin himself actually advised Josiah to wait instead for Watt's steam engine, which he believed would be preferable to his own invention. Similar letters during the following ten years cast fresh light on the introduction of steam-powered mills in the pottery industry, for they make clear that there was a considerable waiting period while Watt perfected his new engine. In 1770 Darwin wrote again: 'Your windmill sleeps at my house, but shall be sent to you, if you wish it, but I should advise you to wait the Wheel-Fire-Engine, which goes on slowly'.[65]

Eventually, in 1779, Darwin finished his plans with their mutual friend Robert Edgeworth, and, according to Meteyard, the windmill was installed at Etruria soon after, though there appears to be no proof of this.[66] What the Wedgwood correspondence and his trial pottery samples do show is that Wedgwood used his windmill – presumably the six-sailed one – along with the other mills for experimenting with different ways of grinding, beginning with hand-grinding small quantities, then using the windmill for larger batches, and finally a water mill for full production, adjusting the formula of his bodies to compensate for the effects of different sources of power.[67]

While the protracted discussions on the horizontal windmill were taking place between Darwin and Wedgwood, steam power made its first appearance in the Potteries. Limitations in the capacity of water mills led to attempts at using steam engines to supplement the natural water power, by pumping water over the existing wheel. Following a visit to Cornwall in 1775, where he saw pumping engines in operation, the potter John Turner introduced a Newcomen engine to his works at Lane End for this purpose. Spode is also known to have installed such an engine at his potworks (formerly the works of Turner) in Stoke at around the same date.[68]

Even this method was limited by the efficiency, relating to water supply, of the original mill, and the only viable solution was to introduce entirely steam-powered mills for grinding flint and colours. The first of these mills appears to have belonged to Josiah Wedgwood. Wedgwood had kept a close eye on developments in steam power, and invited his friend James Watt to tour the potworks in the area where engines had been installed, to gather details of their performance.[69] The visit proved fruitful, for following it Wedgwood ordered his own first steam engine from Boulton and Watt in 1782, and it was erected at Etruria in 1784. It was a Sun and Planet type engine, to be used to power the flint, clay and colour mills. In 1792 Wedgwood decided on a second engine of ten horsepower, which was installed the following year and which, he wrote in a memorandum, was 'To grind flint…To grind Enamel colours in a number of small pans, in the chamber above the flint pan. To work a stamper for pounding our broken saggars…To temper clay'.[70]

The introduction of the mill to the potwork site added an important dimension to the arrangement of the works. It was logical that the mill should be erected where there was direct access to the road or canal from which raw materials could be easily unloaded, and also that it should be situated conveniently for the 'making' shops, though since steam power did not extend to these workshops it was not necessary for there to be any link in the buildings. Aside from this general matter of location, the arrangement of the mill block itself was important, for its plan and design were dictated by the functions for which it was intended. This meant that there was a logical sequence in order of process, and that the power of the steam engine was put to the best and most economical use, with the machinery imposing the heaviest demands in power placed nearest to the engine itself.

The mill at Etruria met all these criteria. Located at the rear of the site, it was out of the way of the main production and the finer processes of pottery-making. At the same time it

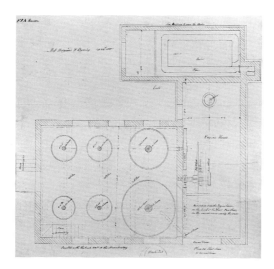

Other details of one of the Etruria mills are known from later descriptions and illustrations.[72] On the ground floor, flint-crushing, a heavy and stress-producing task, took place. A cogwheel raised a vertical shaft and heavy chert stone, which dropped into a large wooden receptacle to crush the calcined flint. On the first floor were the grinding rooms with series of tubs, in which large chert stones were pushed round on a stone bed by wooden arms, with the materials being ground in water. From illustrations it would seem that at least some hand processes were still carried out in the building. Slip was blunged or mixed by hand in tanks, using wooden paddles; clay was also mixed manually.

After blunging, slip was poured into a trough with a fire underneath to evaporate water until the right consistency of clay was reached. The mill was constructed with thick wooden beams, which would be flexible for the strain and weight of mill equipment and movement. There was a hoist for raising and lowering materials between floors. Aside from all the usual components of the mill block, there was a chemist's laboratory in which experiments could take place.[73]

A plan thought to be of a slip house at Etruria suggests that on the larger potwork sites there was more than one such house, or room, for this one was specifically for the flatware section where plates and dishes were made.[74] It also shows the very basic requirements which were necessary for the slip house. Essentially what was necessary was a rectangular room, around the side of which

was not isolated from the communications system, for the canal branch cut out round to the back of the site brought barges filled with flint and other raw materials directly to the door. A plan of 1800, when Josiah Wedgwood II was planning a new engine, produces the clearest, if partial, plan of the mill, showing the relationship of boiler house, engine house and ground-floor pan room with its six pans of varying size, the largest nearest to the engine (Plate 20). Upstairs was a further pan room for grinding colours, a task less demanding on the engine. The main pan room was given additional floor space over one end of the engine house for the convenience of working the crane, which lifted the heavy chert stones used in the grinding pans (Plate 21).[71]

Plate 21
The pan room of the mill block at Etruria in the early twentieth century, showing a flint crusher in the foreground and the brick floor with a stone track for carts

could be fitted the various tubs for mixing, sieving and storing raw materials and slip. The only piece of equipment was a hand-operated pump in the centre of the room, by which the liquid flint and presumably other materials could be pumped through to the main blunger, where all the ingredients would be mixed together.

ANCILLARY TRADES

The mill was just one of the additional facilities ideally required by the major manufacturer by the end of the eighteenth century. The earlier potter had had no need for such buildings or power, and with a very basic method of pottery-making had been quite self-sufficient in production. By this time, however, there was a whole range of ancillary crafts and trades to be accommodated. The degree of self-sufficiency now tended to relate to the scale of enterprise and affluence of the manufacturer, which led to two new features in the industry. One was that the largest potworks were equipped with everything for their purposes, including grinding mills, colour-making areas, kiln furniture, crate-making and saggar-making shops. In some cases these were an integral part of the works, in others they operated as an independent unit on the site: for example, when Spode stopped making decorating materials himself at his Stoke works an outside contractor took on the task, but still on the site.[75] It is also known that Minton was making its own kiln furniture up to the 1830s at least.[76]

The second feature was the emergence of the independent craftsmen and tradesmen. The smaller potter had neither the space nor resources nor the continual need for certain areas in pottery-making or ancillary trades, and turned to either the larger manufacturers or these independent suppliers, while even some of the larger potters chose to contract-out work and make use of outside businesses rather than include them at their works. The 1802 Allbut trade directory shows the extent and range of activity already apparent by the end of the century. Fourteen engravers, eight enamellers, two earthenware gilders and two printers were listed as being engaged in pottery-making. In addition, the Potteries was served by thirty-one lathe makers, six colour manufacturers, a pump maker, two lawn weavers, two canal boat builders and carriers and an oven builder. This is to leave aside the wheelwrights, blacksmiths and ropemakers whose work was used by the pottery industry, and also the whole area of coal mining and the twenty-one coal-masters whose presence was so crucial to pottery manufacture.

Some of the buildings associated with these activities had no special identity, and most are unrecorded. The cratemakers' shops, an important part of the industry, are amongst the exceptions. Photographs show that the larger shops were often long, low single-storeyed brick and tile structures (Plate 22). These were divided into separate workshops, each with its own large fireplace and chimney, giving the effect from a distance of a row of labourers' cottages. There were usually a number of double-doored entrances large enough for the passage of timber and crates, and for loading carts, in between which would be small brick-arched windows. The small independent cratemaker, meanwhile, seems to have worked from his home premises in a very simple workshop.

POTTERY MANUFACTURERS' HOUSES

The presence of all the small concerns, in both pottery-making and associated crafts, is easily lost in the shadow of the relatively few large, prosperous potworks which were already dominating the scene. It was the latter which had effected an improved transport system and widened the markets for pottery. These were the potteries with a full range of facilities, which were becoming directly involved in coal mining and whose manufactories provided copybook examples for the future in architectural style and layout. While the smaller potters were still working as families in the last traces of a cottage industry, these enterprises were heralding the new era in pottery-making and the development of the potworks.

While Etruria dominates eighteenth-century pottery history it must be seen in context, for there were others who were quick to follow Wedgwood's example. The last decades of the century saw the emergence of family-potting dynasties building substantial new pottery manufactories on landed estates. One such family was that of the Adamses, in the northern part of

Plate 22
Cratemakers' shops at Greenfields Pottery, Tunstall, 1960

the Potteries, which had been involved in pot-making since at least the fifteenth century. In the mid seventeenth century, John Adams of the Burslem branch of the family is said to have rebuilt the Brick-House Works, subsequently leased to Wedgwood, changing it from farmhouse to manufactory. His son William inherited the works and took on another manufactory at Cobridge, in 1780 building Cobridge Hall nearby, enclosed in a small park. A second William Adams ran a pottery in St John's Square, Burslem, before also taking on the Greengates works in Tunstall. As well as the potworks, Adams bought a large piece of the surrounding land, on which he too built a 'handsome house' for himself, near to the

works but surrounded by parkland.[77] Further to the east, in 1787, Theophilus Smith of Burslem bought part of the Furlong Estate, demolishing the old house there and building a new house for himself together with a village of (reportedly) forty houses, shops and an inn, and, in 1793, an entire pottery works.[78] Unfortunately, the venture failed and in 1800 Smith was bankrupt.

A more modest development, new but not self-contained, took place at Longport. Formerly consisting of a few cottages, Longport was named in 1777 upon the opening of the canal. The erection of manufactories there was accompanied by the manufacturers' homes and their workers' housing, the complex growing particularly after its

Plate 23
Etruria Hall as originally built, showing the Trent and Mersey Canal in the foreground

Plate 24
Etruria Hall in 1989, with later extensions. The landscaping of its environs was undertaken for the National Garden Festival held in Stoke-on-Trent in 1986

takeover by the Davenport family. Another small community was to develop at Newport, further down the canal, where William Daniel erected a potworks around 1795.[79]

Not all the major pottery manufacturers, however, chose to establish themselves in outlying areas or on rural estates, or to live in isolation from their potworks. In 1789, for example, Enoch Wood built his empire on a site in the centre of Burslem, with his mansion fronting the west face of the works and 'surrounded by convenient pleasure grounds' with views out toward Hanley.[80] Likewise, when Thomas Wolfe erected his manufactory between the Spode works and church in Stoke in 1781, he built his house in the grounds, and in a far less attractive situation than that of Wood.[81]

The earliest surviving example of a manufacturer's house, probably the first of its generation, is the Palladian 'Big House' in Burslem, built for John and Thomas Wedgwood in 1751. This was followed by Joseph Pickford's three-storey Etruria Hall,[82] built for Josiah Wedgwood, the nephew of John and Thomas (Plate 23). Originally of five bays, the accommodation was subsequently increased by the addition of two two-storeyed wings, with single-storeyed links to the main building (Plate 24).

The extension included bedrooms for Wedgwood's children and his assistant, together with a schoolroom and billiard-room.[83] At one stage Wedgwood attempted the manufacture of slates for the roof, and was considering white brick for the building, but this was abandoned in favour of the red brick which was eventually used.[84] The park and gardens surrounding the hall were designed by William Emes, and included a Chinese bridge, summerhouse, dome hovel (to reflect those at the works), fish ponds and nurseries.[85]

Internally, little of the original hall remains intact. A century later Meteyard wrote that 'the principal rooms, opening from a hall which ran the whole length of the house, were large, well-proportioned and lofty. The windows and staircases were ample'.[86] Perhaps the least altered are the cellars, an astonishing labyrinth of small separate rooms extending the length of the house which were used as Wedgwood's private workshops and laboratory. Meteyard described these rooms, where Wedgwood stored his materials 'and made his secret mixtures':

They are a range of cellars shut off from the rest by thick partition walls, and heavy doors.
Wedgwood's means of access was a trap-door, and a flight of narrow brick steps leading from a room which was probably his study. The trap-door steps ended in a wide passage, and from this opened a door to the outer air, as also the cellar in which the mixtures were made, the bins or troughs still remaining. The outpost of this fortress is equally well guarded. It is approached from the rear of the Hall by a double wall screen, forming a sort of winding passage.[87]

It is unfortunate that alterations have wiped away much of the evidence for the appearance of the rest of the house.

The link between interior and ceramic design in the manufacturers' houses is an interesting one. It is known that John Flaxman junior, responsible for the fine designs of Wedgwood's jasper ware, was also employed to design friezes, chimney-pieces, cornices and ceiling paintings for Etruria Hall, between 1781 and 1787.[88] The only description of the interior decoration of the Hall is that 'capacity existed everywhere for the decorative effects of stained glass and terracotta bas-reliefs',[89] but we know also that Angelica Kauffmann was responsible for ceiling decorations,[90] and it is likely that William Blake, a friend of Flaxman, was also involved in the work.[91]

Other manufacturers' houses are recorded as having internal decoration which echoed their

ware. A photograph of a decorated ceiling at Whieldon Grove shows a pattern similar to that used by Thomas Whieldon on his plates, while another ornate plastered ceiling at a late eighteenth-century manufacturer's home, Cannon House, in Hanley (Plate 25), also showed a style which may have been used on the owner's ware.[92] An idea of Flaxman's chimney-pieces at Etruria is suggested in Turner's description of William Adams's house at Greengates, where 'the

Plate 25
An ornate ceiling at Cannon House, a late eighteenth-century manufacturer's house in Hanley

chimney-pieces are of wood and plaster, carved and moulded in the Adam style with wreaths and medallions...Some of the designs are the same as those used on the jasper ware'.[93]

Amongst the most impressive houses built in the Potteries in the period is that said to have been built by John Brindley at Longport (Plate 26),[94] known locally as Dr Mott's House. If this house was indeed Brindley's, then it would have been built around 1773, the year in which he established his potworks, or at least before it was acquired by John Davenport in 1793–4. The

Plate 26
*Dr Mott's House,
Longport*

house, now demolished, was a solidly built brick building with low roof, plain except for a marvellous front portal with pediment and scrolled columns, lavishly decorated with relief fruit and urns, and, above, an ornate bracketed Venetian window.

INDUSTRIAL HOUSING

The industrial population of the Potteries was increasing rapidly throughout this period, from an estimated 7,500 in 1762 to 23,626 in 1801.[95] The accommodation offered by existing cottages was soon outgrown and immediate activity was required to satisfy the new demand for workers' housing. The initial response was to convert and divide a variety of buildings: barns, former potworks and the cottages themselves, but while this subdivision was apparently endless, it was not enough.[96] New building began to take place, with the initiative taken largely by the pottery manufacturers, though there was some involvement by other individuals and also the first signs of building-club activity. Gradually, there occurred the important transition from a scattering of dwellings to organised developments, and from rural cottages to industrial terraced houses. In both planning and architectural design, this period was crucial to the developments which followed in the nineteenth century.

Houses provided by manufacturers

The number of manufacturers involved in providing houses increased, not surprisingly, as the industry grew. It has been noted that Thomas Whieldon owned several cottages by 1750, and the number appears to have increased to around fifty by 1777.[97] Whieldon was unlikely to have been the only potter with such cottages by the mid eighteenth century, though he probably had more than was usual. Several new communities were to be created by the largest manufacturers by the end of the century, the first, largest and best known being that undertaken by Josiah Wedgwood at Etruria around 1770. These were not typical, but while few manufacturers could afford such outlay, the practice of providing houses was quite common by the early nineteenth century. Of forty-seven potters who took out insurance policies between 1789 and 1809, nineteen owned workers' houses, varying from a single cottage to twenty-nine terraced houses. There were others with larger numbers by the latter date, but this sample is probably fairly representative.[98]

It is clear that while many potters provided such houses, the number of employees out of the total workforce to benefit was quite small. The provision of twenty houses loses significance in a potworks employing one or two hundred people, even if several members of a family and household were working there. What, then, was the motivation for building the houses?

Referring to Josiah Wedgwood, in 1865, Llewellyn Jewitt wrote admiringly: 'to be comfortable himself he must know that those around him were comfortable also; to be happy he must impart happiness to others, even the most lowly of his employees; to sit at ease in his new home he must know that those he employed were well and cosily housed'.[99] The sheer beneficence implied by such comments is quite improbable, though philanthropy did play a part amongst those able to afford large developments of housing. What is more evident in the eighteenth century is the value of housing as an incentive to workers. Wedgwood would probably have had difficulty in drawing workers from Burslem to the newly established Etruria, especially during boom periods in the trade. Similarly in Stoke, Spode and Minton needed to lure workers from Burslem, where the main fund of pottery labour was to be found.

Advertisements substantiate this idea of the house as an attraction for the workers: 'Wanted, a journeyman foreman...one who is a good workman, and understands throwing, and is capable of conducting a principal part of the business; he will have a house adjoining the premises, and every convenience, with good wages and encouragement'.[100] What this advertisement also illustrates is that it seems to have been the skilled workers, the higher end of the worker hierarchy, to whom the offer of the limited housing was made. Casual labourers and unskilled workers were more likely to have to find their own accommodation, except in cases where a very large number of houses of differing standards were owned. The other aspect to house provision was that of control. To be favoured with accommodation could be a doubtful advantage, for it carried with it the risk of being evicted for bad behaviour – or indeed for any conduct at work or otherwise which incurred disapproval. The truth behind house provision seems to lie in 'enlightened self-interest' on the part of even the best employer who, while helping to satisfy the demand for houses, could thereby attract skilled workers, draw rents and exercise control outside as well as inside the works.

Most of the developments which took place in this period were still small and fragmentary, taking the form of a single row of cottages or at most a few cottages on each side of a road. By the end of the century, however, there were signs of more complex and bigger groups. The

Plate 27
*Workers' cottages, Lord
Street, Etruria,
photographed in 1946*

developments undertaken by the larger manufacturers consisted of new communities, erected near to their manufactories to accommodate their employees. These would be either rows of terraced housing stretching along the road leading to the manufactory, or more compact groups adjacent to it. At the same time as the manufacturers were building, some of the old estates were being sold off with an eye to housing developments. Usually, the land was divided up into small plots and sold to a wide range of individuals who built independently, but these purchasers were at least controlled by the overall skeletal framework of new streets laid out by the vendor. The resulting developments in Hanley and Shelton, where most activity was taking place, were isolated groups of parallel terraced streets. It is with such streets that the back alley and backyard originated, and from which the most miserable conditions of the following century developed. The disastrous extension of this plan, the court, also made its appearance by the end of the eighteenth century.

The sheer number of houses and scale of building at Etruria was quite revolutionary, but not the type of planning. It was essentially a single-line development, and showed no distinction amongst the bulk of its houses aside from some 'of a better class, for farmers, clerks and others' (Plate 27).[101] There does not seem to have been a more subtle grading either by way of position on the estate or in the houses themselves; in other words, no major social distinctions were made between levels amongst the pottery workers

or between their homes. The development stands clearly in its place in time, at a stage when mass housing was required to accommodate and attract workers but before a sophisticated industrial and urban structure had emerged.

Design and plan

The introduction of planned developments was accompanied by a number of changes in design which distinguished the early industrial dwelling of 1800 from the agricultural cottage a century earlier. Firstly, there was the almost uniform use of brick and tile as opposed to lath, plaster and thatch. Secondly, with brick housing came brick lintels and sills, although wood and stone were also used. Stone as the main building material continued in cottages in the outlying areas of Baddeley Edge and Norton in the nineteenth century, making them appear deceptively early in contrast to the rows of brick terraces in the towns.

The industrial terraced house of the Potteries was usually two-storeyed, there being no tradition of three-storeyed dwellings with integral workrooms (as with, for example, the top shops in textile housing) and no lack of space to encourage the building of multi-storey structures. There were, however, external changes apparent in the new house. The use of brick allowed for more adventurous expression in features and for the first time there was a self-consciousness visible in the structures, and a distinction displayed between the front and back of the dwelling: the house received a social face. In the agricultural cottage there had been no pretensions, but whilst the backs of the early industrial dwellings remained functional and basic, the fronts of some of them were dressed with brick-arched lintels, wooden or stone sills, and occasionally brick dentilling under the eaves of the roof. This did not apply to all: some industrial terraced houses, especially those built speculatively, still had neither back doors nor back windows; or if there were any such windows they tended to be small with only a small part, if any, made to open. The sash window made its appearance around the turn of the century but by no means entirely replaced the casement or fixed type in the cheapest houses.

The most important change in plan came with the extension of the two-roomed cottage to provide a back room on the ground floor and second bedroom above. In terms of size the change was not great, for the new rooms occupied only half the length of the others. The real significance lies in the fact that the new rooms represented the first step in the division of space and function within the home. The agricultural cottage had been entirely communal: in the single downstairs room all family activity took place — washing, cooking, eating and general living; upstairs all shared the same bedroom. With the new plan, the back room became that in which washing and food preparation could take place, with the front room reserved for the more social activities. Upstairs, parents and children were able to sleep separately.

The new arrangement did not immediately affect heating, for fireplaces remained in the front rooms with no heating provided in the back. Cooking continued to be done in the living room, and that room was still the focus of family life. The type and position of the staircase did alter. In the agricultural cottage there had been a corner, spiral staircase, often by the front door, which imposed on living space to the least degree possible. When the cottage was extended the stairs were moved to the back of the house, and by the early nineteenth century emerged from the spiral into a straight, elongated form, which the additional living space allowed and which was also easier and cheaper to construct.

The cottages surviving from this period are in varying states of repair, and some are quite heavily altered. Unfortunately, none of those built by the pottery manufacturers for their workers remain standing, and we have to rely on documentary sources for knowledge of their appearance.

Those built by Wedgwood at Etruria in 1770 were, like the factory, forerunners in new design. The majority had two rooms on the ground floor, two above, with shared outside pumps and shared privies at the end of the back gardens. They were also provided with communal bakehouses.[102] The houses were higher and narrower than previously, with stone sills and lintels to the front windows and hood moulds over the front doors. The houses were demolished earlier this century but photographs show that a small number of them were three-storeyed, which was uncommon in the Potteries. The houses were to suffer from their location in a swampy area by the canal, but when built would have been innovative and desirable as homes compared to existing dwellings.

A clearer picture, and more detailed information, comes from some cottages which were surveyed by the Stoke Historic Buildings Survey and are of interest in showing the type of structures being built at the time. One of the earliest examples of workers' houses, dating from before 1775, is the row of four cottages built near the toll gate on the Newcastle to Trentham turnpike road (Knappers Gate). The end cottage in the row is double-fronted, with five rooms, and was built at a slightly different date from the other three, smaller, dwellings. It is possible that the

owner of the group built first his own, and then the other cottages, and that they were linked to one of the nearby brick and tile works already operating in that area. Such an explanation would fit in with their location and with their superior brick and tile construction, which does not otherwise relate to their quite primitive design.

It is the smaller dwellings in Knappers Gate which are more representative of the ordinary workers' homes. Essentially agricultural cottages with slightly better façades, they possessed brick-arched lintels and wooden sills, and brick dentilling under the eaves. There were no back doors or windows, and therefore no through-ventilation. Each cottage consisted of a single square room downstairs and one above, both of them 13 feet by 13 feet 6 inches (3.9 m x 4.1 m) in size. There was a large fireplace in the ground-floor room, a smaller one above, and it is likely that there was originally a corner staircase. The rooms were not as low as some which have been surveyed and documented in this area, those downstairs being 7 feet 6 inches (2.2 m) and upstairs 8 feet (2.4 m) high. Only the larger, end house had a cellar, the other families presumably storing food in their living rooms or in an outside shelter. It is difficult to say how much garden space there was when the cottages were built, for they predate the canal which runs along the bottom. Nevertheless, the space was still substantial later on, and certainly enough for a degree of self-sufficiency. The families occupying the cottages were out in the country and living in the same environment as the rural labourer, and they were to remain on the fringes of the urban area for a considerable time.

CONCLUSION

By the end of the eighteenth century the massive expansion of the pottery industry, coupled with the rapid growth of the local population, had transformed the area. Settlements which in living memory had been villages were developing into sprawling industrial towns. Canals and turnpike roads had integrated North Staffordshire into the growing web of the national transport system, allowing the importation of ever increasing quantities of raw materials, and opening up the markets of the world to the potters' wares. The Potteries entered the Age of Steam pre-eminent among the pot-making districts, and one of the country's foremost centres of industry.

Chapter 3

THE EARLY NINETEENTH CENTURY: SUCCESS AND EXPANSION

...what a change has public spirit wrought in this interesting tract of country! The ingenuity of the artisan has been seconded by the researches of the mineralogist; and the earth has poured forth her bounties to enrich its owners, and raise the Staffordshire Potteries to the enviable rank which they hold in the commercial world of two continents...

Pitt 1817, p 412

Figure to yourself a tract of country, the surface of which, cut, scarred, burnt, and ploughed up in every direction, displays a heterogeneous mass of hovels and palaces, farmhouses and factories, chapels and churches, canals and coal pits, corn fields and brick-fields, gardens and furnaces, jumbled together in 'the most admired disorder', and you will have a pretty correct idea of the Staffordshire Potteries. Then pervade the space your fancy has thus pictured, with a suffocating smoke, vomited forth incessantly from innumerable fires, and the thing will be complete.

Monthly Magazine, 1 November 1823

By 1800 the pottery industry was well established and expanding, with over 300 potworks.[1] Growth was checked in the early years of the nineteenth century by trade blockades and depression caused by the wars with France and America, though the full impact on the industry is uncertain. The whole question of whether or not the government's Order of Council, which had stopped trade with the Continent, should be repealed, was a political one, leading to a flurry of printed pamphlets in 1812 from those for and against, with different assertions as to the state of the pottery trade. A committee of Staffordshire potters in favour of repeal sent a petition to the House of Commons reporting that 'more than one fifth of our manufactories are unoccupied and falling to decay'. Another manufacturer disputed this committee's claim to represent local potters, and protested at such an alarmist and exaggerated picture, asking 'whether considerable additions have not been made to manufactories, and some new ones erected, to equal, in a great measure, the falling off in others'.[2] At any rate, recovery was soon under way and by the 1820s there was an air of both self-congratulation and optimism.

THE GROWTH OF THE SIX TOWNS

The population continued to increase rapidly, trebling from 23,000 at the turn of the century to 63,000 by 1840.[3] With more and more land needed for both factories and housing, the villages of the area struggled in their individual ways to become industrial towns. The overall impression was one of chaos. One journalist wrote in 1823:

On entering these towns, the first peculiarity that arrests the stranger's attention is the irregular and straggling style in which they are built; for, having most of them sprung up from small beginnings into their present magnitude, in less than half a century, the additions have been made from time to time just as necessity demanded, but without any determinate plan, or the slightest regard to appearance and orderly arrangement. The result has been the strangest confusion that 'tis possible to conceive. Milton's line, 'Wild, without rule or art', was never before half so happily illustrated.[4]

The six centres coped with the transition with varying degrees of success. Tunstall enjoyed a central town plan, set out in 1816 when a group of the main landowners in the area bought a piece of land from Walter Sneyd in order to make a market square. The agreement was made that the land immediately around the square would not be sold to any person of whom the subscribers disapproved, and that the purchasers should be confined to a uniform plan of buildings.[5] Under the control of the landowners, including several manufacturers, the town centre became dominated by a few large manufactories. The Malabar plan of 1848 shows that the land surrounding the town was still owned by these same individuals, while the area immediately around the square was sold to various purchasers: Paradise and Piccadilly Street to the Tunstall Building Society, Amicable Street to the Tunstall Sick Club, and the southern side of the market-place to Charles Hulse, a joiner and builder.[6]

Tunstall managed to maintain a higher degree of order than its neighbours partly because it was a comparatively new town unfettered by old housing and irregular property boundaries, partly because of the rules laid down in 1816, and also partly because of the domination of the centre by potworks. It was only in the 1870s, with the demolition of the Pinnox Pottery, that the whole of the area to the immediate north of the square was opened up to building development, by which time experience in urban planning, together with improved housing standards, allowed the rational development of uniform terraced streets.

As the oldest centre of potting, Burslem had a legacy of houses and potworks accumulated over the centuries, around which it expanded in haphazard fashion as land was released by the major landowners. Such housing development as took place was dictated by the large potworks which were situated in the centre of the town, while the most ordered groups of housing were built outside this area, where there was space.

By 1800 Hanley and Shelton together exceeded Burslem in population. The pottery and mining industries had attracted an increasing number of workers, and the two townships were already emerging as a commercial centre. In the late 1780s the first, large planned housing development, the initiative of the local potter and landowner, John Mare, had begun along the road to Stoke,[7] and in 1806 a second plan incorporated the whole of the southern part of the modern town centre, based on the cross formed by Piccadilly and Pall Mall.[8] While this development was gradually being filled in with housing and shops, building clubs were at work to the north and south.[9] The potworks of Hanley were more widely scattered than elsewhere in the area, although the majority tended to be located in the centre.

The town of Stoke was already dominated by several large manufactories when in 1793 a local landowner, John Ward Hassells, laid out its main streets and modern centre. In that year, his grandfather had died, leaving him land in Stoke. Hassells immediately began laying out streets on the land, and divided the area into building plots for sale. The enterprise was carried out with the collaboration of ten trustees for the roads, who were probably involved in the plan from the

outset. Five were major pottery manufacturers in the area: Minton, Spode, Wolfe, Booth and Rowley. All of them bought plots of land from Hassells, together with six others, and some were involved with another agreement which Hassells made on a central site for the erection of a market-hall and schoolroom.[10] Each plot was quickly filled in, mainly with small groups of terraced houses, alongside earlier dwellings. There was no overall planning and the area became densely packed with fragmentary groups, its cramped backwaters creating some of the most miserable living conditions as the century progressed.

Fenton grew from three separate settlements, remaining fragmented and without a centre to the end of the nineteenth century, when landowner and manufacturer William Meath Baker was responsible for the creation of a new, single town centre around a town hall and other civic buildings. Fenton's reputation as a pottery town was based on a relatively small number of large factories built at intervals along the Stoke to Longton road.

A latecomer to industrialisation, Longton grew the most quickly (and without plan), inside the confines of land released by the two major estates of Heathcote and Sutherland during the 1780s. It had a much higher proportion of small potworks than, for example, Stoke. While in the latter the large manufactories and housing retained some separation, in Longton houses and manufactories became tightly enmeshed. The long main road leading from Stoke to Meir was deceptive in hiding a maze of small irregular streets bulging with potworks and houses. In 1829 Simeon Shaw, writing when growth was still in its infancy, noted the improvements which had occurred:

> For many years it was notable for the great irregularity in the position of its buildings; of every size and sort, from the respectable residence of the manufacturer, to the mud and saggar-hovel of the pauper, scattered over a wide extent of territory. But in comparatively recent times, under the almost magic influence of a prosperous manufacture, improvement has commenced, the buildings are regular in size and position, and the place has risen into a respectable station in the scale of Staffordshire Towns...[11]

He was probably impressed by the main, fronting road, however, for behind this the town was developing rapidly in a tightly confined space with a mass of smaller potworks and housing, and it soon gained a reputation as a warren of industrial chaos and despair.

Plate 28
*A backyard scene in
Longton, with bottle ovens
and factories towering over
the adjacent terraced houses
(photograph taken in the
1920s)*

Though the majority of new potworks continued to be sited in the town centres, increasing numbers were being built along the area's expanding road and canal systems. By the early nineteenth century, the transport system was further improved by the introduction of tramways linking collieries, canals and roads, offering more scope for the location of potworks. Especially useful was the tramway linking Longton and Stoke. One manufactory was advertised for sale in 1806, for example, with the advantage of

> *...the ready delivery of Coals, by a Railway,
> within 40 yards of the Pit's Mouth, even without
> the assistance of a Horse. This singular advantage
> in a consumption of 40 tons of coal per week,
> would render a direct saving of £150 per annum.
> And as a Railway is now laid from Lane End to
> Stoke, the necessity of keeping a team of horses for
> this manufactory will be completely obviated.[12]*

In existing centres, the groupings of potworks and housing merged to create an uneven patchwork of development. Where the potworks were built in outlying areas new communities emerged, in some cases identified with a single manufactory, such as Dale Hall in Burslem, and Greendock in Longton.

Behind the gloss of celebration which accompanied the emergence of the Potteries and the area's new-found opulence, the reality of industrialisation was quite different. Building areas were restricted by estate ownership, and in the tight-knit communities which developed, potworks and houses competed for space (Plate 28). There was little concern for the quality of the environment, or distinction between land suitable for industrial development and for housing, even for high-class residences. In 1801, for example, part of the Goats Head Estate at Cliff Bank, Stoke, was offered for sale as 'one of the most flourishing parts of the Staffordshire Potteries, and presenting a building situation, either for Houses for the residence of genteel families, the erection of Potworks, or other buildings, not to be met with in any part of the populous and still increasing neighbourhood'.[13] Similarly, glebe land around the new church in Stoke was advertised in 1827 as being 'eligible for the Erection of Houses, Manufactories, and other Buildings, and for Wharfs, Quays, and other conveniences for the Purposes of Trade and Commerce'.[14]

The industry therefore ruled, and pre-occupation with its growth together with inexperience in urban planning ensured that the situation would quickly deteriorate. It was already becoming severe, with signs of the confusion, ugliness and pollution of later years. As one visitor in 1823 wrote:

> *The contrasts of meanness and magnificence which
> meet the view are...striking; the humble hut of the*

artisan stands in immediate contrast with the palace of his employer, and splendid mansions rear their heads amid the sulphurous fumes and vapours of the reeking potworks. Everything, in short, announces that appearances are here quite a secondary consideration when opposed to utility, and that the genius of industry alone presides; taste and elegance in the buildings are therefore but little cherished at present.[15]

MANUFACTURERS' HOUSES

The larger manufacturers were accumulating capital, while at the same time the pressure of space was such that their old houses on the potworks sites were either absorbed or swept away to make room for more workshops. For both reasons, some of the more affluent manufacturers moved away from the grime which they had created to houses which they built in more pleasant, open surroundings at a distance from their works.

It is of little surprise that the country estate continued to be an aspiration of many manufacturers, but the idea of the estate as a self-contained industrial community did not develop from the previous generation's potters. Instead,

those manufacturers who were able and chose to purchase an estate did so only to provide themselves with a home and a pleasant environment, not to include in it their manufactory or houses for their employees. Thus, while old rural estates were taken over by pottery manufacturers, they were not converted to industrial use but remained in isolation, acting as further restrictions on urban development. In some cases the estate was only rented, as that at Golden Hill, Fenton, which was let by the landowner John Smith, first to Jacob Marsh of the Boundary Works and then to John King Knight of the Foley Potteries, during the early nineteenth century. Both manufactories were a convenient distance from Golden Hill House and park, but quite isolated from them by landscape and situation.

A variety of styles seems to have been adopted for the new houses built by manufacturers. One of those still surviving, the Palladian Portland House in Burslem, was built in the early years of the nineteenth century and occupied by the Riley family (Plate 29). The ground-floor windows, set into arched recesses, recall John and Richard Riley's Hill Works in nearby Westport Road, rebuilt in 1814. A quite

Plate 29
Portland House, Burslem, built for the Riley family in the early nineteenth century. The front porch and side bay were added later

Plate 30
Bank House, Burslem,
built in 1828 for Richard
Riley, the manufacturer

different style was chosen by Richard Riley when he built Bank House for himself, further out of Burslem, in 1828. Demolished in 1987, this was a tall, two-storeyed, stuccoed house in the Gothick style, with slender corner turrets and crenellated parapets (Plate 30).

One of the most important surviving examples of the country house and estate is The Mount, in Penkhull, purchased by Josiah Spode at the turn of the century (Plates 31 and 32).[16] When Spode bought the estate it was to build his own home in a parkland retreat; his potworks remained in the centre of Stoke and his employees were dispersed throughout the area.

The Mount is a two-storeyed, neo-classical house, designed in two parts, with a narrow bridging section: the main house was for the family, and the smaller building accommodated the servants and service area. The centrepiece of the whole is the stone colonnaded bow at the front of the house, surmounted by a dome, which forms the main entrance, flanked by two pairs of tall sash windows.

The grandeur of the frontage is continued into the two-storey main hall, topped by a glass dome and beyond into an oval hall, which mirrors the front bow. The main effect internally was

achieved by the arched alcoves in the halls and in the billiard-room, each beautifully formed with decorative shell and feather moulding. The stone staircase off the main hall was equally fine, with an ornamental wrought-iron banister. Other features of the house are the carved door surrounds, arched corridor entrances and moulded borders throughout, some added later but others original.

The accommodation which the house offered was, in contrast to the reception area, relatively simple and moderate in space. Unfortunately, all the fireplaces, probably the focus for decorative treatment, have been taken out. At the end towards the servants' quarters were the breakfast-room and dining-room, with the drawing-room and billiard-room to the other side of the halls. Upstairs were five bedrooms, the master-bedroom above the drawing-room.

The servants' house was altogether more modest. A central corridor ran the length of the house, with, at the front, the pantry, servants' hall, housekeeper's room and, in the bridging section nearest the family's quarters, the butler's pantry. At the rear of the house were the scullery, kitchen and larder and, across from the butler's pantry, the small servants' staircase. Upstairs were seven bedrooms. Below the bridging section of the

house and spreading into the main building were vaulted cellars, approached by the servants' stair.

Estates such as The Mount were important but they were in the minority. In fact, the noticeable and perhaps surprising discovery is that so many manufacturers, upon taking over businesses, remained in the town centres in the houses attached to their works. Their priority was apparently to use their capital to build up the business rather than to erect a country seat at some distance away. Hence Zachariah Boyle and Son lived in the house inherited with the eighteenth-century potworks of Thomas Wolfe, in Stoke, and Richard Hicks stayed at the White House belonging to the old Baddeley potworks in Hanley, his partner Meigh living at the nearby Albion House before eventually moving further out of the urban area. The distastefulness of the industrial environment by this date should not be overstated, for much of the Potteries was still relatively rural. Nevertheless, it is clear that the manufacturers who chose to remain there were subjected to the increasing by-products of their industry. In 1829, Simeon Shaw described the Boyles' house as 'large and handsome...but most injudiciously situated in the midst of manu-factories, whose smoke necessarily proved a

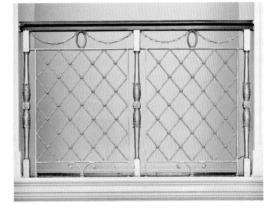

continual source of annoyance'.[17] Ingenuity and imagination were shown even in such urban settings. The house of the Longton manufacturer J Carey was described by Shaw as rather

elegant, and has its appearance improved by being placed on an island in a large reservoir, that supplies condensing water for the Steam Engine at the Mill, where are ground flour and the various materials and colours for the manufactories; and when the engine is working, a single jet fountain throws up warm water several feet high. There are a beautiful small bridge, gates, large cannons, etc.

Plate 31
The Mount, Penkhull, built for Josiah Spode

Plate 32
The Mount, Penkhull: detail of ornate iron balustrade

He ended on a disappointing note, however: 'the whole is exposed to the smoke of the manufactories'.[18]

WORKERS' HOUSING

As the description of the emerging town centres has suggested, the areas of workers' housing were mainly scattered and small in scale, in groups between potworks or on land which became available on the fringes of the existing communities. The hierarchy of workers was becoming increasingly complex and sophisticated, from managers and foremen to the highly skilled designers, modellers and engravers, through the ranks of throwers to others in the 'making' processes and the firemen, to warehouse and unskilled labourers and 'odd men', down to the lowest paid, the women. This was to be reflected in the houses in which the workers could afford to live, groups of which were distinguished from each other by size, facilities and architectural detail.

Design and plan

In the early decades, the form emerged which would remain the basic plan for the worker's house to the end of the century. The builder had become more conscious of economy and space, and increasingly concerned with the number of houses he could fit in a row. As a result, the width

of individual houses decreased, though at the same time there was an increase in their height. The architect had not yet become involved: the prime concern was for economy, and the construction of 'boxes' in which to house the expanding working population. But as the gradations of the social hierarchy developed, Georgian decorative and structural details – tall sash windows, stone sills and lintels, panelled doors and porticos – began to appear. These, rather than the overall design, reflected differences in status, and indicated the changing contemporary fashions passed down from superior domestic architecture.

Internally, several new features developed during this period. While the dimensions of the front room were reduced, additional space was provided by enlarging the back room to an almost equal size. At the same time, ceiling heights were raised to 8 feet or 8 feet 6 inches (2.4 m to 2.6 m). As the back room became larger, so it was possible to build the staircase along its side, rather than in a tight corner spiral. Later on, a fireplace was introduced into the back room of the better-quality house, enabling cooking to be done there. Chimney-breasts were scaled down in size, and chimney-stacks were narrower than during the earlier period when they had served large open fireplaces.

Finally, as the internal area of the house increased, so the size of the garden dwindled until

Plate 33
*Seven Row, Penkhull,
built by Josiah Spode
c1803*

families no longer had a plot on which they could grow vegetables, but only a small confined backyard. Many early industrial dwellings still had garden space, and even at the height of industrialisation there were some comparatively rural spots where this was still so. On the whole, however, the back garden disappeared and communal, subdivided garden plots emerged as a feature of the towns, on spare ground at a distance from the houses themselves. Segregation had become a feature of external as well as internal space, fully reflecting contemporary concern for privacy and possessions. The price of a slightly larger, compartmented house was the confinement and pollution of the industrial town.

Housing provided by manufacturers

The pottery manufacturers continued to be involved in providing housing for their employees, not undertaking single large developments but accumulating groups of houses over a number of years. In some instances, the provision was a token one for key workers, as appears to have been the case with the group of eight houses owned and possibly erected by Hicks and Meigh between 1806 and 1812 to replace earlier cottages belonging to the old Baddeley Pottery on Broad

Street, Shelton. The remains of these survive, heavily altered by conversion to shop use, but still possessing moulded round-headed doors which suggest that they were a relatively superior group, offered to the more fortunate of the workforce. Most potters possessed no more than ten workers' dwellings, but some of the large manufacturers were to erect streets of housing amounting to thirty or forty dwellings. Josiah Spode chose a number of small developments. Around 1803 he provided forty-eight houses in Penkhull, but in separate groups, including the 'Seven Row' and 'Ten Row'. A surviving photograph (Plate 33) shows the former to have been a neat row of brick and tile cottages, simple and unadorned.

More interesting architecturally is the courtyard development which he then erected in the centre of Penkhull, known as 'Penkhull Square' (Plate 34). The single arched coach entrance into the cobbled yard of the court, and the plain brick and tile buildings, made it very reminiscent of the courtyard potworks. Only the dwellings fronting the road side had their frontages facing the outside; those on the other three sides of the court faced inwards. At the front were casement windows, at the back tiny sashes, those on the ground floor adjoining the plain

Plate 34
Penkhull Square, a courtyard housing development provided by Josiah Spode

Plate 35
Building-club houses, John Street, Hanley, 1807

wooden doors and sharing their brick-arched lintel. The cottages were two-up, two-down in plan, with the narrow rear room characteristic of late eighteenth-century dwellings, from which a corner spiral staircase led up to the first floor. There was just one fireplace, in the front downstairs room. Communal privies were in the central shared courtyard.

In some instances the industrialists appear to have encouraged self-help amongst their workers rather than erecting houses themselves. Enoch Wood was said to have been responsible for initiating a development known as Fountain Buildings on Newport Lane, Burslem, which was built by his workers 'without the aid of building society, land society, or socialist scheme'.[19] The group, also called Tuppenny Row, consisted of twenty terraced houses, ten on each side of a central shop.

Building clubs

In whatever form, however, the number of houses which the manufacturers were providing for their workers in the first decades of the century was only a small proportion of the whole. Much greater activity came from speculators and building clubs, particularly the latter, which were not only responsible for some of the most fully planned developments and a very large number of terraced dwellings (Plate 35), but led the way in providing a superior quality and type of house. Whereas the houses supplied by the manufacturers ranged from the best to the worst in the Potteries, those built by the clubs were, with exceptions, at the forefront of design and played an important part in raising standards of workers' housing and in the early development of the towns.

The earliest recorded building club is the Thistley Field Club in Hanley, formed in 1797, but it was during the following three decades that building clubs were the most active. Seventeen building clubs or societies are known to have been at work during that time, and there were probably many more. They were run by a small number of trustees, who organised monthly meetings for members. The trustees were mainly well-to-do tradesmen and craftsmen, while members were from a wider occupational range, including some of the better-paid pottery workers. Of the sample of clubs for which details are known, an average of only 28 per cent of the members became owner-occupiers, the rest letting their houses to tenants.[20] The main purpose of the early societies in the Potteries was not to allow working men to own their own homes, but rather was a means of investment for the growing number of individuals with a modest amount of spare money.

Subscriptions raised a part of the money required; the rest was found by obtaining a mortgage from a variety of private sources. The developments undertaken usually consisted of a single street or two streets, on which a certain number of houses were built per year, and lots drawn to decide on the order of priority. When all the houses had been built and the financial business completed, the clubs were terminated.

There is sufficient information on the early building clubs, from both surviving houses and documentary sources, to provide one of the liveliest images of building activity in the Potteries.[21] Of particular relevance here is the type of houses being built by the clubs, in so far as they accommodated the better-off pottery employees and provided a model for subsequent workers' housing. A survey of those erected by the Tunstall Building Society between 1816 and 1822 serves as illustration.[22] The society had bought a piece of land adjoining the newly formed market square, on which it laid out Paradise Street and Piccadilly Street. The development consisted of forty-six houses along the two parallel streets, with a cobbled alley running between. Apart from two smaller dwellings, the houses were two-up, two-down in plan, the front rooms being 13 feet wide by 11 feet 6 inches deep (3.7 m by 3.4 m) and the scullery and back bedroom 10 feet 6 inches by 10 feet (3.2 m by 3m). Fireplaces were provided in each of the downstairs rooms, and possibly in the front bedroom at least, while the staircase was placed along the side wall of the scullery and led up to a small landing upstairs. The back door opened on to a small yard, at the end of which was a privy and ash pit (the provision of individual privies was unfamiliar to the ordinary worker's house). The yard walls were high, respecting the new tendency toward private, self-contained units as opposed to communal areas. A passageway half way down the street gave access through to the back alley, and provided at least some ventilation.

The superiority of these dwellings was made clear to the outside world on the street front. Because of the increase in height, the houses were able to adopt Georgian features which gave them a certain amount of distinction in comparison with the usual frontage. The sash windows were quite large, 5 feet high by 3 feet wide (1.5 m by 0.9 m), with stone lintels and sills, while the door had moulded classical surrounds.

The example set by houses of this quality was to be followed by others over the next two decades with little further advancement. Around the same core design, there were variations in size and facilities and in the degree of external ornamentation, according to the status of the house. It was not until the middle of the century, however, that the next step forward was made.

FACTORY LEGISLATION AND THE POTTERY INDUSTRY

While the pottery manufacturers were content that other agencies should share in the task of providing homes for their expanding workforce, they were far from eager to relinquish any degree of control over their manufactures and industry to any outside body. Astonishingly, the pottery industry was to remain outside the Factory Acts for sixty years. Government awareness of the problems of industrialisation, especially of child labour, had brought the first regulatory act in 1802, but this act related only to the cotton industry, where the abuses were first brought to light. The pottery industry was included in the 1816 and 1833 Parliamentary inquiries into conditions in factories, and was known to hold similar evils. In 1818, one Member of Parliament pointed out that the potteries as well as the cotton manufactories had children working long hours, 'but no remedy had been applied to them'. Why, he asked, 'if the evil was admitted to be the same in both cases, was not the same remedy applied?'[23] It was a matter of priority in the face of an overwhelming task, and one which was approached hesitantly and cautiously, with many interested Members of Parliament reluctant and opposed to intervention. Although pottery manufacturing had become for the most part a factory-based rather than a domestic industry, it defied definition in terms of factory legislation, in many cases taking place in small workshops which were free from powered machinery. Above all, in the initial inquiries it was felt that the manufacturers were a benevolent and 'intelligent class of men',[24] who were capable of supervising the industry themselves. Not surprisingly, while their progress and fine establishments were being acclaimed, the manufacturers did their best to

Plate 36
Interior of Spode factory,
Stoke-on-Trent, showing
cast-iron fire-proof
construction

on child labour and from external interference in general. The assertion that the pottery industry was entirely the affair of the masters and men was in practice unfounded, since it was the former who controlled developments. The over-riding effect of government non-intervention was that little change occurred in the Potteries, except that working conditions were allowed to worsen.

THE DESIGN AND CONSTRUCTION OF POTWORKS

The question of fire-proofing in pottery architecture is of particular relevance in this period, with what seems to be the first preventive measures taken in the design and construction of the potworks.

Despite the recognised vulnerability of thatched roofs, it was not until the 1740s that the first brick and tile potworks was said to have been built. The potters Thomas and John Wedgwood, we are told, 'incurred great censure because of their extravagance in erecting so large a manufactory and covering it with tiles, (all others being covered with thatch...)'.[26] Gradually, over the following decades, more and more thatched roofs were replaced with tiles, not only in potworks but in all types of building. It was a slow transition, and partially thatched potworks are recorded in insurance policies as late as 1816.[27] Where these buildings are specified, they include warehouses, workshops, a dipping house, saggar house, plate house, packing house, and even a hovel shed. Even more surprisingly, thatched potwork buildings do not seem to have incurred a higher premium than tiled ones: when the thatch was replaced by tiles at the Mellor potworks in Shelton in 1806, for example, the buildings continued to be insured at the same rate.[28] Nevertheless, the gradual change from thatch to tiles was almost certainly influenced by the recognition of the former's susceptibility, as well as to contemporary changes in building style.

A construction of brick and tiles, with wooden framework, was the norm by the early nineteenth century. The exact date for the introduction of iron into potworks is unknown. The use of structural iron to reduce the risk of fire as pioneered by Charles Bage in his flax mill at Shrewsbury in 1796–7, and by Strutt in his Derbyshire mills, was slow to be taken up in the Potteries.[29] The earliest surviving evidence of fire-proofing is to be seen at the Spode factory in Stoke and the Price and Kensington Pottery at Longport. Early nineteenth-century buildings at Spode have brick-arched ceilings on the ground floor supported by cast-iron columns supporting

encourage the image of a primitive industry: an acknowledgement of the term 'factory' would only draw unwelcome attention and bring forward their inclusion in legislation and governmental control. At a Committee of Inquiry in 1816, Josiah Wedgwood II maintained that his buildings at Etruria were very different from those of cotton works and other manufactories in which machinery supplied the power. They were, he argued, 'very irregular, and very much scattered, covering a great space of ground and, in general, only of two storeys in height'.[25] Such a description belies the organised system and arrangement of Etruria, but the idea it conveyed was quite reasonable for the mass of small concerns.

The Potteries fared increasingly badly in the investigations which preceded each factory act, but emerged each time still free from restrictions

Plate 37
Groin-vaulted basement mould store, Spode factory

cast-iron beams with wrought-iron tie rods (Plate 36). A feature of the columns is the series of slots punched along their length, so that shelves could be fitted between them. The most interesting arrangement is in one of the two earliest surviving buildings on the Spode site, in a basement used as a mould store, where there is a fine example of groined vaulting stretching the length of the building (Plate 37).

Outside influence seems to have been fairly slow in filtering through, though it is known from a letter written by Josiah Wedgwood II to Charles Bage in 1813 that he at least was aware of what had been occurring elsewhere. The letter concerned advice about a building at Etruria:

You were so good as to say you would favour me with the proper proportions for iron beams for flooring with arches...The building is 36 by 31 feet clear inside measure. The beam might be supported in 2 places to make the bearing 10ft. 4ins. I shall be very much obliged by your instructions for the beams and for the span and rise of the arches – if that would be economical – the support will be iron pillars 9ft. high.[30]

The building in question is thought to be the packed crate shed, where crates full of ware ready for despatch were stored and so were of particular importance with regard to fire protection. Unfortunately, there is no other surviving correspondence between Wedgwood and Bage, but the tone of this letter suggests that it was a serious proposition that was carried through.

A similar construction may also have been used in Mason's new factory in Fenton (1815–20),

Plate 38
Hill Works (now Wade Heath factory), built by John and Richard Riley in 1814

Plate 39
Detail of the central pedimented bay of the Hill Works. Although now much modified, the arched coach entrance and sash windows, dressed with stone, are typical features of the architectural style adopted for potworks in the early nineteenth century

where the front warehouse was described as fire-proof.[31] In cases like this four-storeyed range, this type of construction would also have been used for its load-bearing strength, though it occurs even in small two-storeyed buildings at Spode and in the early nineteenth-century Boston Pottery at Newfield.

The absence of iron in the majority of potworks, when the technique had become common in the textile mills, may have something to do with lack of communication with these other industries, and also with its greater cost and complexity in building. On the other hand, it may simply be that the compartmentalisation of potworks was a reasonably adequate means of fire protection, if not preventing fires then at least containing them. A study of contemporary newspaper reports has suggested that the pot ovens (by now known as 'bottle ovens' on account of their distinctive shape) were less likely to be the immediate cause of fires than poor building construction and carelessness. It has also been suggested that the damage was not often catastrophic, but confined – presumably because of the separation of workshops – to specific areas.[32]

THE DEVELOPMENT OF AN ARCHITECTURAL STYLE

In the first decades of the nineteenth century, the erection of big new manufactories and their fully developed bottle ovens proclaimed the success and growth of the industry. The model introduced by the previous generation of potters became fully established and refined, and it is the buildings of this era that display most simply and clearly the features typical of industrial pottery architecture.

The façade

The style and standard of building at the front of the potworks differed greatly from what lay behind. The façade took on the role of advertising and was appropriately impressive: any architectural embellishment was concentrated on this public face, and the most was made of whatever presentation the site allowed. Generally, the display was confined to the front of the building, but where the sides could be seen from the road they too were given superior details. The few corner sites which were developed were similarly treated, with the central pedimented bay as the corner feature. Such a plan, already used by Enoch Wood in Burslem, was copied by John and Richard Riley at their new potworks further along Westport Road in 1814, now occupied by Wade Heath (Plate 38).

The formula established by Etruria and other late eighteenth-century works was almost universally adopted by the next generation. The long frontage with central pedimented bay, arched coach entrance with stone dressing, quite large, evenly spaced sash windows with stone lintels and sills, all became standard features (Plate 39). There was often brick dentilling under the eaves, and it was also used to highlight the pediment. Most striking of all was the uniform addition of the central Venetian window, which had become one of the strongest symbols of pottery architecture (Plates 40 and 41). The frontages as a whole were often remarkably alike, suggesting that manu-facturers took careful note of other new potworks when erecting their own, and used copybook patterns of design which passed from hand to hand amongst the builders.

Behind the façade

In contrast to the façade, the rest of the works was utterly plain and functional, with series of small-paned, wooden-silled windows, and crude, simple doors. Internally, the front range, which housed the offices and showrooms, usually had plastered walls and ceilings, panelled doors, light rooms, and fireplaces and fittings of superior quality. The workshops behind were bare, unplastered shells, those on the upper floors with wooden frame-work exposed. The front range had by far the most pleasant environment and the most elevated status of the works. This was the area which visitors saw, and in which the administration of the works was carried out. It may also have been where the élite of the workers, the modellers, designers, engravers and gilders, were accommodated. As a journalist was to write of the Spode factory in 1846: 'The modellers' and engravers' apartments...evidence an attention to the comfort of the occupants, deserving of the highest praise in the proprietors.' It was an attention that was completely absent from the workshop areas of the manufactories.[33] Both internally and externally, the social hierarchy of the pottery workers and of the outside world was reflected in the buildings which they respectively worked in and visited.

It was usual to adopt a single, large courtyard plan rather than clusters of small courtyards. No one had a site as extensive as Etruria, and few were using such a range of clay bodies as Wedgwood. A single quadrangle was less expensive, and was more efficient for a less ambitious range of production. Not all potworks were based around a courtyard, and when they were it was not necessarily symmetrical or quadrangular – much depended on the site and on its background. These features were the basic and model ones, however, which the ideal premises would allow. The enclosed plan provided a form of security for the premises, and easy monitoring of entry and departure.

As the manufacturer chose to build his house away from the works, and as security and surveillance became a more important consideration, the idea of having a lodgekeeper resident on the premises was born, with a cottage next to or containing the lodge office itself (see above, p 24).

The problem of stealing from sites was evident early on and was included in measures to deal with local theft in general. When an association for the prosecution of felons was formed in Burslem and Tunstall, in 1808, among the main categories incurring penalties were the theft of earthenware, colour and utensils from manufactories, and the members of the association were largely pottery manufacturers in the area.

The manufactory was arranged so that production began at the rear and finished at the front of the premises. Thus all the dirtiest stages of the process, and those dealing with large amounts of material – preparation and grinding, saggar-making and slip-making – took place at the back of the site. Here they were furthest from view and would make use of any rear access, either road or canal, for bringing in raw material. The 'making' and decorating shops were in the rear three ranges

Plate 40
The first-floor Venetian window on the front of Mason's Ironstone Works, Hanley

Plate 41
The nearly identical Venetian window at the Greenfields Pottery in Tunstall

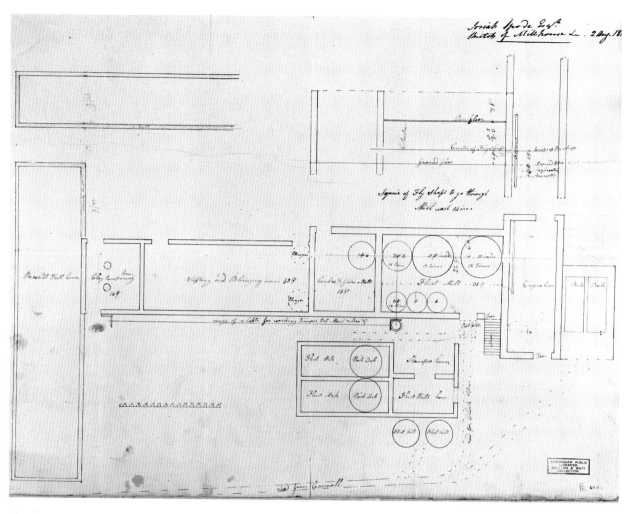

Plate 42

Plan of steam-powered mill proposed for Josiah Spode's works, 1810, by Boulton and Watt

of the quadrangle so as to allow for the cross-movement of the ware made necessary by the different, sometimes overlapping, stages and treatments of production. This was a very important aspect of potwork planning. Although there was an overall forward movement, the complex sequence in the making process ruled out any purely linear arrangement. To rationalise and maximise efficiency fully in the potworks was difficult, and though smooth-running production was achieved in them, the problem came to the fore later in the century when the industry fell behind others. The ovens were in the main courtyard area, either within or at the back of the courtyard, allowing easy access for the several firings. The front range was occupied by the cleanest and final stages in production, that is packing and warehousing, and also, as noted above, by the élite of the works.

Usually the potworks were of two, sometimes three storeys, and were served mainly by external staircases. A surviving four-storeyed building at the Spode Works has a narrow, partly wooden and partly stone staircase running up the interior rear wall with openings on to each level. None of the other earliest surviving structures has such stairs, though they are all of two storeys, even where such a design was not particularly suitable.

Some potworks are known to have had basements, where conditions were often particularly dismal. The potter Charles Shaw remembered working in the basement of the Hill Pottery during the 1840s:

> It was a long, narrow cellar... At the lower end of the basement storey was the throwing room, in which two throwers worked, and at the back of this was the 'stove', in which the ware was dried. No daylight ever directly penetrated this place, being built below the surrounding earth, and only lit by the stove fire.

> On the line of the throwers' room there ran in front of the high road the turners' room, from thirty to forty yards in length, filled with lathes, and at the back of it another dismal dungeon, called a

cellar, for the green ware brought from the thrower's stove or drying-room. Beyond the turners' room, still fronting the road, there were the handlers' rooms, connected by a dark, narrow passage, called 'The Purgatory', which ran underneath a grand entrance to the bank. The first handlers' shop was partly occupied by six young women who made 'stilts', or pot triangles, to put between pieces of flat ware in firing, so as to prevent cohesion. There was another handlers' shop in which a man and two boys worked; and 'the top hopper', a small dark den, with little light and no ventilation, sometimes used by stilt-makers and sometimes by handle-makers. All these latter shops were much below the high road, and were damp, dismal, stuffy holes, with little light even at midsummer. They always had a close, mouldy smell, as the only entrance to them was a deep, narrow staircase, some twenty steps deep. A similar entrance, some fifty or sixty yards away, led down to the turners' room.[34]

It seems that basements were not commonly used as workshops, however. It was more usual for them to hold waste clay, or to accommodate slip areas for mixing liquid clay, or to be used as mould stores. Where such an arrangement was possible, they might also provide a damp store for green ware. In the Price and Kensington Pottery there is a vaulted chamber of this sort at ground level, like a large tunnel, into which ware is taken on trolleys, the floor flooded with water, to prevent unfinished ware from drying out during potters' holidays.

THE USE OF STEAM POWER

The eighteenth-century potters' experimentation with steam power was consolidated in the nineteenth century, though still confined mainly to the preparation areas of the manufactories. Surviving plans of the mill designed by Boulton and Watt for Josiah Spode in 1810 show an idea in arrangement and function similar to other contemporary mills in the Potteries (Plate 42).[35] The complex was laid out so that the most logical order in the sequence of processes could be followed, and for the most efficient and practical accommodation of steam power and machinery.

In a small separate area attached to one side of the main mill block, flint was calcined or burnt in a kiln, then crushed by a stamper, and washed ready for the next stage. The main building was arranged with rooms in a line, ordered according to the degree of power which they required. At one end were the boiler house and engine house. Next was the two-storeyed flint mill, with a shaft room on the ground floor serving the pan floor

above: the large flint-grinding pans made the heaviest demands on the engine. The main shaft then led through the colour and glaze-grinding mill where it powered further grinding tubs, and finally led to the third processing room, where sifting of materials and blunging or mixing of slip took place. Meanwhile, a subsidiary arm of the shaft was fed through the side wall of the flint mill along the length of the others to the clay tempering house, where the clay body itself was mixed ready for use. The mechanisation of such mills as this, so fully geared to industrialisation, stood in strong contrast to the hand craft which held sway in the pot-making departments of the works.

ORGANISATION OF THE WORKFORCE

Except for some of the general 'making' areas and the warehouses, the workshops were small with relatively few workers in each. In 1833, for example, it was reported that at Ridgway's Cauldon Place porcelain works there were not more than four to seven people employed in most rooms, though in one there were twenty-two girls, in another seventeen.[36] Workers were still strictly segregated. With more open information on clay and glaze recipes and techniques, there was less obsession with trade secrets by this time. Nevertheless, the fragmentary nature of production remained, and so did the manufacturers' interest in control.

There were also new motives for segregation. One of these was a genuine fear of moral corruption, especially amongst social philanthropists and critics of the factory system, who condemned the practice of having large numbers working together on the grounds that it fostered immoral conduct. This was reflected in many types of building, significantly applying as much to the workhouse as to the potworks, with a similar but even greater obsession about separating males and females, adults and children.

A second motive for separation may have been a desire on the part of the manufacturers to discourage organisation amongst the workers. External political affairs in the late eighteenth and early nineteenth centuries did not leave the Potteries untouched. Worker-consciousness developed amongst the potters at an early date, and in 1824 the first organisation, the Journeyman Potters' Union, was formed. Conflict between workers and manufacturers became an increasing occurrence and was to give rise to serious and bitter confrontations. In the view of manufacturers, the less opportunity employees had to discuss their grievances the better, and while the moral and skill factors were put forward by the manufacturers, it is very likely that reasons of discipline and isolation were prominent in their minds.[37]

Mason's Ironstone Works

One of the potworks to survive from this date, Mason's Ironstone on Broad Street, Hanley, illustrates all of the general points of pottery architecture and discipline made above.[38] The manufactory stands on the site of the old Baddeley works on Broad Street, Hanley. The Baddeleys offered their business for sale in 1801, as a 'roomy and well-built set of potworks' with a piece of land behind 'abounding with saggar marl and Brick Clay of the first quality'. This land, Pool Field, provided a good supply of water; there were also collieries within a short distance of the works, and the site was well placed by the main highway. A substantial house built by John Baddeley stood in front of the works, and there

were 'eight dwelling houses at a small distance, very convenient for the workmen employed in the manufactory'.[39] The works was finally sold to Richard Hicks and Job Meigh who, while recognising and valuing the assets of the location, by 1815 had rebuilt the potworks to provide an establishment geared to the requirements of nineteenth-century industry (Plate 43). On its three-acre (1.2-ha) site the new works was one of the largest in Hanley and Shelton, employing around 600 workers by the 1830s.[40]

The situation of the manufacturer's house at the front meant that it reduced the full visual impact of the façade, which was nevertheless an impressive one. The front range was very long, two-storeyed, with a central pedimented bay accommodating the familiar Venetian window with an oval date plaque above. The pediment was accentuated by brick dentilling and a continuation of the banding at the corners to suggest the full triangular shape. There were two rows of evenly spaced sash windows on each side, with stone string coursing dividing the upper and lower storeys (Plates 43 and 44).

Unusually, the main entrance to the works was not at the front but at the side, where there was probably a lodge, with the addition later of a lodgekeeper's house.[41] From here the lodgekeeper could overlook all movement and register the workers' arrival and departure. The stables appear to have been in an adjoining building at one end of the front range, and the rounded corner of the lodge allowed ease of turning for carts as they approached. The side entrance was the only one in an otherwise completely enclosed courtyard. A further opening at the rear of the site allowed the transport of raw materials but this access was restricted to the preparation areas behind the main courtyard.

The manufactory had a symmetrical courtyard plan with similar movement of ware to that described above. The buildings at the rear of the site were near the source of water and marl and accessible for the conveyance of materials via the rear entrance. Here slip-making, saggar-making and the preparation of materials took place. In the rear, on two sides of the quadrangle, were the 'making' and decorating departments, while in the front range were warehouses on the ground floor, offices above. By 1841 the works were said to consist of sixty rooms and five offices.[42] When built there would have been no machinery in the actual pottery-making areas, so that there were relatively small workshops, separated according to the many different stages of production. The work rooms were unplastered, and those on the upper floor had their wooden roof structure exposed.

Plate 43
The front elevation of Mason's Ironstone Works, Broad Street, Hanley, 1815

Entrance to these upper floors was by external staircase, laying all movement open to observation and easing congestion. The rooms had small-paned windows, as numerous as, but smaller than, those at the front of the manufactory. In 1815, when the government was seeking income to help finance its foreign policy, there were proposals to levy tax on factory windows, which Hicks and his fellow manufacturers protested against as 'oppressive, impolitic, unfair and unequal'.[43] The was not carried out, and the number of windows remained unthreatened and unlimited in factory design.

The owners discouraged familiarity amongst their workers, any sharing of experiences and any opportunity for immoral behaviour. In 1841 Hannah Fenton, a 33-year-old supervisor in the painting section, was in charge of the apprentice girls' department, which accommodated twenty-three girls aged from eleven to seventeen years. They were 'kept quite apart from all the rest of the people and in no case associate with the boys...There is a fine if either should interfere with the other'. Hannah herself could not be sure about wages in the biscuit-painting room, 'as I have never been there, nor have I in any other than the three departments in my life'.[44]

The rooms were supplied with fireplaces and pot stoves. Temperatures varied. The painting rooms may have been 'warm, but not uncomfortably warm', but the drying stoves in the 'making' department (in some manufactories heated up to between 120° and 140°F) gave the young mould runners extremes of temperature to contend with, which, together with the steam from the drying moulds and ware, made it 'very rare you find a man of forty-five' if he had spent years in the section. Poor ventilation was most unhealthy, not only in this department but also in the painting rooms, where noxious decorating materials were used. Hannah Fenton observed that 'The tar is strong; the only effect I have ever

Plate 44
Mason's Ironstone Works

observed is that it creates an appetite.' She maintained that the children were quite healthy, though there were 'two cases of swelled neck'.

There were no separate rooms for eating. Those living further afield ate their dinner in the workrooms, using the pot stoves, and were open to contamination from the decorating and glazing material. The risk of poisoning was further heightened by the lack of any proper washing facilities other than a trough in the courtyard. One of the dippers told of having suffered from glaze dipping, with his hands constantly in contact with the lead glazes: 'My hands have been drawn up, and I have suffered great pain. I think it is an unhealthy occupation. I am a father of a family, and as a father I would never bring my boys up in the dipping house.'[45]

The works was reported as being 'well-drained, and lighted by candles'. The hours worked were from 6 am to 6 pm in the summer, 7 am to 6 pm in the winter, which were standard hours for many of the manufactories, but meant that natural light for close work would have been quite inadequate. The ranges had windows on both sides, but workers on the ground floor would have been poorly served in the enclosed courtyard arrangement.

A bell inside the main entrance summoned the employees to work. Not all manufactories had their own bell, and until 1829 in Hanley at least, the bells in neighbouring chapels were rung in their stead.[46] In the same way, the pottery workers used the clocks of chapels and town halls to get them to work on time, though problems of variance constantly caused trouble. These practices were all part of the closely interlinking relationships between employer and worker, manufactory and community, in everyday life.

By the early part of the century Longton was quickly catching up with Burslem and Hanley as a potting community, with potters from the other areas taking advantage of available land and opportunity. The communications network was sufficiently developed; there was no canal, but the roads were turnpiked and a horse-drawn railway linked Lane End with Stoke wharf. With the manufacture of earthenware already established in the other centres, it was in Longton that the production of bone china became prominent, together with the cheaper wares of nineteenth-century industry.

Plate 45
The front elevation of the Boundary Works, Longton

Plate 46
Entrance to the Boundary Works

The release of land during the 1780s by the trustees of Obadiah Lane, lord of the Manor of Longton, together with that allowed by the Marquis of Stafford, helped generate this activity but also confined it to a ribbon development along the turnpike road. The resulting thread of development contributed to the local description of Longton as the 'neck end' of the Potteries, and is still visible today in the striking line of factory frontages that extends along the main road through Fenton and Longton.

The Boundary Works

One of the Longton potworks dating from this period is the Boundary or California Works along Church Street, only the front range of which survives complete (Plate 45).[47] In 1818 the Duke of Sutherland leased a plot of land on the south side of Church Street in Longton to Jacob Marsh, for a term of ninety-nine years at an annual rent of £3.[48] From a long line of potters, Marsh had moved from Burslem to set up his business in Lane Delph in 1806, since which time he had obviously been sufficiently successful to embark on building his own new factory designed specifically to his requirements. Within a year of taking the lease of this land just inside the boundary of Longton, he had built the appropriately named Boundary Works, which first he and then his son were to occupy for almost twenty years.[49]

Marsh's factory was designed on a courtyard plan. Its most noticeable feature was its extended, oblong shape which allowed the maximum street frontage, and thereby maximum space for the presentational aspect of the works. The brick and tile façade was symmetrical, with eight bays either side of a larger central bay which formed the main entrance to the works. The outer six bays on each side were of two storeys, while the middle section rose to three storeys with a tapered roof and central gable. The central bay had a key-stoned arch, Venetian window above and Diocletian window underneath the gable (Plate 46). The other stone-lintelled and silled windows were evenly spaced, and each storey was marked by stone string-coursing; matching dormer windows were provided on the third storey. There was brick dentilling under the eaves along the entire length of the frontage, and a datestone above the central lunar window as a final touch.

Inside the front range traces of the storage racks remain on the first floor which, apparently one long room, was a warehouse and display area. It had plastered walls and ceiling, and relief mouldings in a similar vein to those of the later Foley Potteries a little way down the road. Neither the ground floor nor top floor were thus furnished; it seems most likely that the former was also used for warehousing and packing. Alterations have made it impossible to say if there were fireplaces on the first two floors, though the survival of those on the top floor make it seem likely. (It may be, on the other hand, that only the top floor was thus heated, and occupied by designers, while the warehousing was unheated.)

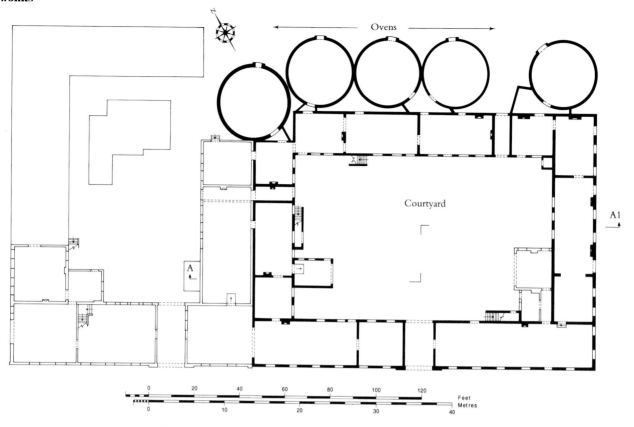

Ovens

Courtyard

A

A1

Feet
Metres

Figure 1
Foley Potteries, Fenton

1a *ground-floor plan*

One office was tucked behind the front range, and there were possibly more in the main building. This separate room may have been a supervisor's since it overlooked all areas of the works. Another 'office' to the north of the front range was present at least by 1857, seemingly that of a lodgekeeper since a weighing-machine stood before it in the road. Since the central cart entrance was the only one to the street, there would have been another such room to one side of it in the front range, past which workers would enter and be clocked-in. Demolition and alteration have wiped out doors, windows and staircases, but we know that there were the usual external staircases to upper floors in the front and north side ranges, while in the front range there was also an internal staircase at each end, and another leading from the first to the second floor.

Behind this front range the works were less symmetrical or orderly, though they did surround a courtyard. The layout of the factory was arranged in standard fashion, with the manufacturing process beginning at the rear of the site and ending at the front, with cross-movement in between. The marl house was situated appropriately nearest to the marl bank, with the slip house next to it. Unfortunately, maps do not give information more specific than 'workshops' for the side ranges, except that the rear end of the southern side was being used as a painting shop by 1857. None of these buildings survives, so it is impossible to make any assumptions about them.

The Foley Potteries

At the same time as Longton was emerging as a pottery town, the main road between Longton and Stoke was also a focal point for large new manufactories, centred at Fenton where collieries provided abundant supplies of coal. The Foley Potteries, demolished in 1983, was built on the

1b *front elevation*

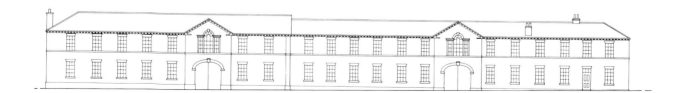

road further along from the Boundary Works between Fenton and Longton around 1827 by landowner John Smith, in a speculative venture uncommon amongst the traditional local landed gentry (Figure 1 and Plate 47).[50] The Smith family had owned the larger part of Fenton for the last century, and although by 1829 John Smith had moved away from the family seat at Great Fenton Hall to Elmhurst near Lichfield, he retained the family's property in the Potteries.[51] Given the extent of this, it is not surprising that the site chosen for the pottery was an excellent one. It was in an undeveloped area between the townships of Fenton and Longton, but on the main road between Stoke and Longton and on the route of a mineral line between the two areas; thus there was room for a spacious factory which could be further developed, with resources at the rear of the site, and well situated for the transport of raw materials and despatch of wares.

The Foley Potteries had a simple rectangular courtyard plan, but, as its five bottle ovens indicate, was built to support a substantial concern (Figure 1a). Smith let the factory from the start, but although not directly involved with it, he ensured that it would be a monument to the family's status. It was built of brick with stone dressings and tiled roof. The long front range (Figure 1b) was set back from the road, its façade a copybook grand design, symmetrically arranged and with a slightly advanced central gable which held the arched, key-stoned coach entrance to the factory. Above the latter was a central Venetian window, while, set in six bays to each side, the other windows had glazing bars, flat stuccoed lintels and stone sills. There was a band of stone string-coursing between the upper and lower storeys, and brick dentils to the eaves and gables. The side elevations (which could also be seen from the road) had identical features, with the

Plate 47
The Foley Potteries, Fenton, in 1961

Figure 1
Foley Potteries, Fenton

1c *section A–A1*

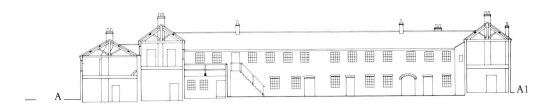

same windows and string-coursing, in keeping with the front. The factory was a showpiece to the passer-by. Once through the inner courtyard, however, a quite different picture was to be seen (Figure 1c). The windows shared only their regular spacing with those of the outer elevation, their panes were smaller, the lintels of brick and sills of wood, and no decorative features whatsoever were evident within the working area.

It is impossible now to say with certainty how successfully the factory was designed for its purpose, though at the time it was regarded as a 'modern and very complete works.'[52] Like other large potteries of the time, it had, in addition to the customary buildings, its own steam-powered flint mill at the rear of the site.[53] The mill area comprised the mill itself and the engine house, together with buildings, presumably used in the preparatory stages of production. There may have been a marl pit to the rear of the site supplying saggar marl, with the saggar house nearby. The slip house was in the area, which was approached by a cart entrance along the eastern side of the factory.

Thus the first and dirtiest stages of production took place at the rear of the site, furthest from the road and from the public eye. Possibly some of the shops in this part were used in the making of pots, since they were convenient for the line of ovens. Four of the five bottle ovens seem originally to have been grouped in a semicircular arrangement at the rear of the main courtyard complex, but later all stood in a line along the same space. They were not enclosed in placing sheds, but covered ways linked them with the rear range, so that ware could be carried straight through under cover; these covered ways would also have provided shelter for firemen tending the ovens. On the other side, the ovens were open to a second courtyard bounded by buildings in the mill area. It is probable that there were 'making' shops on one side of the main, front complex, using areas for biscuit firing on that side, while ware passed to the other side to the glazing/decorating shops and thence to the glost kilns.

The three working ranges were very plain, two-storeyed structures, as was the rear side of the front range. Heating was provided by open fires in every room. There was access between each, but the only communication between floors was by outside staircases in the courtyard, which meant that workers and ware could pass to the upper floors without going through the ground-floor shops. There were only three of these staircases, however, one of those at the front range, so that there would have been much tramping through other rooms.

The rooms in the front range were as dissimilar to those in the working ranges as the façade was to the rest of the works. The western part of the ground floor was as other parts of the factory, and was probably used for packing and despatching wares. At the other end were offices, with plastered walls and covered ceilings. Upstairs, a warehousing/display room ran the whole length of the building, again with plastered walls and ceilings, and lined with fitted wooden racks for displaying the firm's ware.

Both proprietors and their products soon established a reputation for superiority: the former were referred to as 'gentlemen of the most respectable character as tradesmen and members of civil society', while the pots they were producing were 'better classes of willow pattern and other blue printed services', superior in their quality and having 'attained celebrity in the markets'.[54] The factory itself, under the scrutiny of the Children's Employment Commissioner in 1841, was reported to be 'modern, well-constructed, open, roomy, and in all respects good'.[55]

The arrangement of the factory was quite possibly efficient and deemed suitable for production purposes. For the workers, other than perhaps those in the offices and showrooms, the conditions by modern standards were far less favourable, with poor lighting, no ventilation, no evidence of washing or proper toilet facilities, and the exposures to extremes of temperature inherent in all of the potteries.

As a result of the factory's success, and possibly the need for a separate area for china production – the firm was making china as well as earthenware by the 1830s – between 1832 and 1849 a new set of buildings was erected, adjoining the original factory on its western side, but comprising a quite distinct and very similar courtyard pottery.[56] The new part conformed to the original in both style and symmetry, indicating what little architectural change had taken place in the intervening years.

An interesting postscript to this period is the plan produced in 1839 by Andrew Ure, in his *Dictionary of Arts, Manufacturer and Mines* (Plate 48).[57] Ure describes the Staffordshire pottery as being

usually built as a quadrangle, each side being about 100 feet long, the walls 10 feet high and the ridge of the roof 5 feet more. The base of the edifice consists of a bed of bricks, 18 inches high and 16 inches thick; upon which a mud wall in a wooden frame, called pisé, is raised. Cellars are formed in front of the buildings, as depots for the pastes prepared in the establishment. The wall of the yard or court is 9 feet high and 18 inches thick.

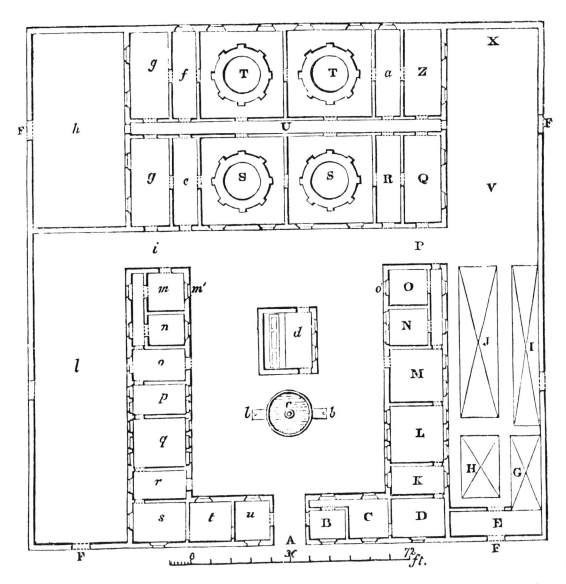

Plate 48
*Plan of a Staffordshire
pottery (Ure 1839)*

The reference to mud walls and seemingly to only one storey make this an outdated description, but the plan which Ure includes, with its detailed layout, nevertheless gives a useful reference point in any study of the courtyard pottery. In this model, the lodge house and counting house are in the front range, as is one of the warehouses and three workshops.

The intrusion of workshops into the front range appears to have occurred in other potworks, and the mould-maker's shop still has its place there at the Price and Kensington works in Longport. The collection of 'making' shops forms the two sides of the quadrangle, with the biscuit and glost ovens, dipping house and warehouses at the back. The muffle kiln for enamelling and the water pumps are situated in the centre of the courtyard. At this pottery there is extra space down each side of the main quadrangle, used for all aspects of manufacture outside the actual

making process. Thus a quarter is designated for slip preparation, a quarter for the storage of clay, hay and straw in wooden sheds, an area for the carpenter, packing and the smith's forge, further storage areas for clay, saggar clay and the saggars themselves; and finally a space allowed for extra workshops that might be needed in the future. In reality, the area outside the quadrangle varied considerably from one potworks to another. Many sites were constrained to the extent that their quadrangle walls formed the boundary, while others had spare ground on which to expand at a later date. What Ure's plan captures, when used in conjunction with building evidence which survives, is not only the potteries' very rigid courtyard structure, but also the fluidity of the arrangement within the basic design, which is able to cater for the size and shape of site together with the particular workshop requirements of the different manufacturers.

Chapter 4

THE MID NINETEENTH CENTURY: THE PRICE OF INDUSTRIALISATION

On approaching from Newcastle under Lyme, Burslem and Hanley appear upon an eminence, and the prospect that presents itself is one of the most extraordinary I ever saw; it consists of an extensive line of what has the appearance of regular fortifications rising before you. The adjacent hills are covered with the lofty columns and large pyramids of chimneys and with the great round furnaces, of which dozens are seen grouped together, like a vast chain of gigantic bomb mortars. The lofty roofs of the drying-houses, the spacious warehouses, and the massy walls enclosing the whole establishments or workhouse bank, as it is called, with piles of clay, flint, bones, cinders, and other materials, serve to complete the illusion.

Kohl 1845, pp 37–8

He raises large dens for the confinement and slow murder of his fellows, and calls them factories.

Undated extract given in Burchill and Ross 1977, p 35

There were fluctuations in the progress of the pottery industry, and in the fortunes of its manufacturers. There were always those able to take over the potworks of failed entrepreneurs, however, and despite the economic depression in the 1840s, expansion continued. In 1851 there were still over 150 china and earthenware manufactories, employing around 20,000 workers.[1] The industry was at its most intense in terms of production and in its domination of the towns, and its impact on the local environment, landscape and population was only now becoming fully apparent. A peak was reached, not only of success and achievement, but also of pollution and human misery.

EXPANSION OF THE POTWORKS

For the many manufacturers without the money or inclination radically to alter their works, expansion was a piecemeal affair. On restricted sites and with limited finance it meant filling in the old courtyards and adding buildings as money was available, for whatever purposes were required. This often had the effect of destroying not only whatever symmetry there had been, but also efficiency and rationality in the order of production. The ovens and hovels, whose lifespan was relatively short, were constantly being re-paired, rebuilt and added to in number wherever there was space on the site. Along with the new buildings, bottle ovens sprang up everywhere, rising out from, or peering over, the roofs of

potwork buildings in a wide assortment of bottle shapes. This lack of uniformity and order gave the impression of an almost organic growth, and increased the pot ovens' visual impact on the outsider.

In all cases expansion took place on the original site. In the smaller works, confined in cramped premises, the result was a hotchpotch of structures squeezed into the space. One toy manufactory employing around twelve people was described as:

a curiosity in structure and management. It was rusty and grim. As to form, it might have been brought in cart-loads from the broken-down cottages on the opposite side of the street. The workshops were neither square, nor round, nor oblong. They were a jumble of the oddest imaginable kind, and if there had been the ordinary number of workshops on an average-sized pot-works, placed as these were placed, it would have been impossible to have found the way in and the way out. As it was, though so small, it was rather difficult.[2]

In larger works, and those occupying a greater space, the result was the same but with more possibility of retaining a sense of order. Such was the old Spode Works at Stoke (Plate 49), which from 1833 was owned by Copeland and Garret:

There is quite a labyrinth of courts and passages, bounded by buildings in every direction, so that it is difficult to obtain a clear idea of the arrangement of

Plate 49
*An earthenware model of
the Spode Works, based
on a plan drawn in 1833*

*the place. The buildings themselves, however, are
definite enough in their appropriation. In many
cases the whole of the buildings surrounding one
court, or quadrangle, are appropriated to one kind
of work, and the group, or square, is named
accordingly: thus there are the plate-square, the
saucer-square, the dish-square, and so forth...*[3]

The state of the industry's architecture appears to
have been one of confusion, much of it, as
Charles Shaw was to recall in 1903, made up of
'ramshackle conglomerations of buildings, as if a
stampede of old cottages had been arrested in their
march'.[4]

The successful production and popularity of
bone china led an increasing number of potters to
become involved in its manufacture, mainly in
conjunction with their earthenware businesses. To
do so meant enlarging and reorganising their
works, as happened at the Foley Pottery, where
the similarity of old and new potworks was often
striking.

ARCHITECTURAL STYLES FOR POTWORKS' FAÇADES

Architectural attention, unsurprisingly, continued
to be focused on the frontages, with little evidence

of concern for the works behind. When George
Coxon was employed to redesign the Phoenix
Pottery on Broad Street, Hanley, in 1845, it was
the elevations rather than the works which were
praised as 'one of the chief ornaments of that part
of town, and highly creditable to the good taste
and skill of Mr Coxon'.[5]

Those who were prospering and could afford
to spend money on their manufactories did so.
Variation in architectural style, from the standard
to the flamboyant and extravagant, is more
notable in this period than any other.
Furthermore, with increasing restrictions on space,
and the rising price of land, a trend towards
building upwards rather than sideways began: large
works became awesome and intimidating. Even
so, the general impression is one of architectural
conservatism. None of the frontages was
remarkable for its progressiveness, only for
eccentricity, and even then the tendency was to
incorporate the same traditional features of central
bay, basket arch, pediment and Venetian window.

Among the most ornate works frontages of
the period were those of the Hill Pottery in
Burslem and the Edensor Pottery in Longton, the
former fictionalised as the building which decided
Edwin Clayhanger on his career as an architect, in
Arnold Bennett's *Clayhanger*. The Hill Pottery was

Plate 50
*The Hill Pottery,
Burslem, rebuilt for
Samuel Alcock in 1839
and described at the time
as 'the most striking and
ornamental object of its
kind within the precincts
of the borough' (from
Ward 1843)*

Plate 51
*The Hill Pottery: detail
of the front entrance*

rebuilt for Samuel Alcock in 1839 by a Shelton architect, Thomas Stanley (Plates 50 and 51). Stanley is known to have designed St John's Church and school in Goldenhill, and St Thomas's Church in Mow Cop, none of which could have been further removed from his work for Alcock.[6] The street range of the works had the by now traditional Venetian window with pediment over. There, however, the similarities ended; the façade being far more ornate than those of any of its predecessors, the decoration was designed to focus attention on the near central entrance bay. This emphasis was provided by an unusually elaborate entrance, surmounted by a tall Venetian stair window, pediment and cupola with flag-pole. The entrance was flanked by pairs of fluted Ionic columns which supported the projecting ends of the first-floor balcony.

The entrance itself took the form of a tripartite opening, echoing the Venetian window above. In contrast, the treatment of the bays to either side of the entrance was relatively restrained, ornamentation being restricted to the chamfered stone voussoirs of the ground and second-floor windows, and the hood moulds of the first-floor window.

Most potteries from this period show the traditional simplicity and restraint characteristic of the industry's architecture, with few concessions being made to the more ornate styles becoming increasingly popular among the builders of commercial buildings. The new Phoenix Pottery was the same as any earlier works except for a parapet and for the introduction of recessed blank arches on the ground floor with inset windows. This arcading, reminiscent of other industrial architecture of the nineteenth century, was to appear in a number of manufactories of this period, though it never became a predominant feature.

WORKING CONDITIONS IN THE POTWORKS

Some manufacturers continued a close daily involvement with their manufactories, while others became personally as well as physically more remote. Their concern about the works and conditions within them also varied. In 1841, the government commissioned a major investigation into the employment of children in factories, which for the first time considered the potworks in terms other than their suitability for pot-making. Commissioner Samuel Scriven divided the works into three categories:

In the first class, I have inserted all those manufactories of most recent structure; many of them are built upon scales of great magnitude, in some instances of beauty; among these may be mentioned the Messrs. Minton and Boyles, Alcocks, and John Ridgways; they contain large, well ventilated, light, airy, commodious rooms, in all respects adapted to the nature of the processes carried on in them.

The second class form by far the most numerous, and are of greater or less extent, having from 50 to 88 hands engaged; most of them have been erected many years, and as the trade increased, so the rooms appear to have increased in a corresponding ratio. Some here and there, upon, around, and about the first premises, so that there is neither order, regularity, nor proportion; the consequence of this is, that men, women, and children are to be seen passing in and out, to and fro, to their respective departments all hours of the day, no matter what the weather, warm, cold, wet, or dry; the rooms, with very few exceptions, are either low, damp, close, small, dark, hot, dirty, ill ventilated, or unwholesome, or have all these disadvantages.

The third class, which include the Egyptian-ware and figure manufactories are even still worse; but the children to be found in them are very few, and in many of them there are none. In eight cases out of ten of the whole, the places of convenience for the sexes are indecently and disgustingly exposed and filthy. It has throughout appeared to be most strange that masters should have paid so little regard to this offence against decorum and morality;

in some places the women and girls are compelled to pass through the hovels where men and boys of the lowest character work, to relieve the calls of nature; others sit under the same shed slightly partitioned off, exposed to the vulgar gaze of half the men on the premises, to avoid which the better disposed either wait their return home, perhaps, at some considerable distance, or run to some opposite, or next door neighbour for relief; independent of the immoral and debasing tendency to which this neglect gives rise, their impurities and unwholesomeness are evident.[7]

The conditions of individual factories varied. In Burslem, for example, they ranged from Cork and Concliff's Egyptian Ware factory, which was described as 'a miserably dilapidated building in which the people work, being low, ill-ventilated, dirty, hot and unwholesome', to Alcock's earthenware and china factory which Scriven found to be 'one of the largest and best conducted in the Potteries'. Good conditions did not necessarily go with the size of the works. William and Samuel Edge's factory in Fenton was described as 'small, but in excellent order. The rooms are large, open, and in every respect comfortable'; while the large-scale Adams works in Stoke 'were of the most ancient in the district, extending over 12 or 14 acres of ground, and situated in the lowest part of the town; the rooms throughout are in a very dilapidated condition, as well as close, damp, hot, dirty and uncomfortable'.[8]

The attitude to the general dilapidation and anarchic arrangement of the older works was summed up by Thomas Shelley, who worked at the Boyle factory in Stoke: 'you must take them as they were built'.[9] More specific problems and grievances, of which the workers were only too aware, and which received the strongest criticism from Scriven, came through quite clearly in the Commission investigations, however. Concerning the stoves in the making department, Scriven reported:

These hot houses are rooms within rooms, closely confined except at the door, and without windows. In the centre stands a large cast iron stove, heated to redness, increasing the temperature often to 130 degrees. I have burst two thermometers at that point. During this inclement season I have seen these boys running to and fro on errands, or to their dinners, without stockings, shoes, or jackets, and with perspiration standing on their foreheads, after labouring like little slaves, with the mercury 20 degrees below freezing. The results of such transitions are soon realised, and many die of consumption, asthma, and acute inflammations.[10]

Plate 52
'The Dipper' (mid nineteenth-century stereoscope photograph)

Similar health risks were involved for those working between the tremendous heat of the bottle ovens and the open courtyard. The question of ventilation was raised in regard to all parts of the works, not only because of the extremes of heat and countering draughts, but also the clay and glaze dust throughout, the dust produced by scouring, and the fumes from enamel paints (Plates 52 and 53). The potworks' hygiene facilities were equally inadequate. Many had shared, makeshift toilets exposed to all, and where there was reasonable provision, particular note was made of the fact. There were no washrooms, even for those working with lead glazes, but only pumps in the courtyards.

Twenty years later the problems were critical. Especial attention was paid to Longton, the town most recently industrialised and with the largest percentage of workmen turned manufacturers who, with only limited means, were unable to carry out improvements on their rented premises. The landlords were said to be 'either too poor to improve them, or are unwilling to keep pace with the times, affirming that the old times were the best, and that what did for them might do well enough for those that came after them'.[11] The government inspector, Robert Baker, pointed out that while his report concentrated on Longton, there were 'banks [potworks] as bad, and potters as vicious' in each of the other areas.[12] His discoveries were horrifying:

The Banks have indeed been formed, in many instances, of old premises rude in construction,

Plate 53
'The Paintress and Edger'
(mid nineteenth-century
stereoscope photograph)

unevenly built, and of all sorts, sizes and shapes, background and foreground blending in grotesque confusion; and having been added to from time to time as the necessity arose for greater accommodation, they now resemble huge rabbit burrows rather than manufactories; for they are in and out, up and down, underground and attic, up rickety stairs and down storage cellars requiring a firm step and an aptitude to stoop, and a sharp eye to enable one to see round all corners, for the creatures, young and old, male and female, which are running here and there, in every direction.[13]

Specific problems ranged from the lack of paving in courtyards, to employees working in intense heat in rooms built around the oven hovels.[14] In his summary report in 1862, the commissioner,

Mr Longe, quoted the surgeon and mayor of Hanley in his statement that pottery employment was 'one of the most deleterious and destructive of human life in the country', made so 'by the faulty construction, imperfect ventilation, and over-crowding of the workshops'. Dr Arlidge, senior physician at the North Staffordshire Infirmary, shared his view: 'The potters as a class, both men and women, but more especially the former, represent a degenerated population, both physically and morally. They are as a rule stunted in growth, ill-shaped, and frequently ill-formed in the chest; they become prematurely old, and are certainly short-lived.'[15] The toll on workers had become intolerable, and it could not be denied that the potworks themselves were at least partly responsible.

THE USE OF MACHINERY IN THE POTWORKS

The pottery industry made only very limited use of machinery. Many of the smaller works had none at all, and in the larger ones, machinery was confined to the preparation areas, where it dominated planning and structural considerations. Elsewhere in the works it had little influence. Even on the 14-acre (5.7-ha) Spode site, apart from the mill, steam power, by 1841, was used only for two throwing wheels and ten lathes, while the boilers supplied steam for heating a green house, throwing house and turning house.[16] In 1844 Charles Mason introduced the Jolley Machine into his Fenton manufactory, but was forced to abandon it. The machine, designed to be operated both by steam and by hand, reduced the labour force required from six men to one man and a boy, and thus was greeted with immediate opposition from the workers.[17] There were in any case technical difficulties with it. Pottery-making required machinery capable of considerable delicacy, suitable for a variety of clay bodies and types of ware, and it was found that the jigger and jolleying machine produced hair-cracks in the backs of nearly all the ware produced by that method. Trade union organiser William Evans doubted that the defect would ever be overcome: 'some of the most practical men of the trade believe that no mechanical appliance can ever remedy the evil…The ductibility of clay requires more than a fixed and immovable tool to fashion the ware. Human touch and skill are required.'[18]

It would have needed a large incentive for the manufacturer to spend time and money on the development and introduction of machinery; even for those who could afford it, such incentive was lacking while there was a cheap and ample source of labour, especially that of children. In 1861 there were 4,605 children under the age of ten working in the potworks, that is almost 14 per cent of the total number of pottery employees. Of this number, 593 were children of five years old, and over a half were girls.[19] It was the children who did the most mundane tasks which might have been replaced by automotive power. As a result, though manufactories grew larger to take in more of the individual hand-operated pieces of equipment, there was no need to consider steam power or automatic machinery.

The question of machinery has a bearing on issues of organisation, economy and discipline. According to Charles Shaw, the absence of machinery contributed to the general inefficiency of the potworks:

Machinery means discipline in industrial operations. In the Potteries there was no such discipline, and very little of any other. I write of what I saw, and of conditions under which I and others worked. Owing, as I believe, to the absence of machinery, there was no effective economical management of a pot-works. Economical occupation of the premises was hardly ever thought of. 'Cost of production', as determined by all the elements of production, was as remote as political economy in Saturn. There was only the loosest daily or weekly supervision of the workpeople, in their separate 'shops', and working by 'piece-work', they could work or play very much as they pleased. The weekly production of each worker was not scanned as it was in a cotton mill.[20]

He further asserted, in remembering his working days, that the anarchic potwork structures themselves helped break down the system of discipline which had been established earlier:

Some of the 'banks' had very few square yards of open spaces. There were tortuous ways round 'hovels' and under archways…so that many of the workshops were separated one from another as if, virtually, they were miles apart. This condition hindered any common rivalry in production, and led to many forms of dissipation and idleness which could never have occurred with larger intercourse. It also prevented any effective inspection by the bailee of the habits of the workpeople in each shop.[21]

Whatever laxity and inefficiency was fostered in such workshops, one thing is certain. Conditions in them were appalling; the pots themselves were paramount, the human requirements of those making them disregarded.

THE IMPACT OF FACTORY LEGISLATION

Change came at last when the government included the pottery industry in the 1864 Factory Acts Extension Act, for this outside intervention had direct effect both on the industry itself and on potwork architecture. It was the pottery manufacturers themselves who finally petitioned Parliament for legislation to control the employment of young children – 'the first body of manufacturers who had themselves sought to inflict this restrictive legislation on their trade'.[22] Some of the most affluent and influential manufacturers were amongst the twenty-six who signed the petition, for example, Minton, Wedgwood, Ridgway and Adams, and they could best survive any intervention which government legislation would involve. Their argument was that child employment was 'the cause of various moral and physical evils to the youthful population', and that the situation could be altered only by a government commission, since few of the manufacturers could be brought to agree to a change.[23] Those opposed to legislation argued that it would prevent making up lost time on orders, that in a half-time system for children it would be difficult to organise relays, and that families badly needed the extra money provided by their children's employment. One manufacturer told the Commissioner, Mr Longe: 'I am strongly opposed to any legislative interference, I think that in our case we are quite competent to manage our own affairs'. Longe tried the thermometer on a stove in the manufactory concerned and found the heat to be 120°F.[24]

The implications of legislation for the earthenware and china industry were that maximum working hours were restricted to ten; no child under eight years was to work in the factories, and those under thirteen should spend half a day in school to each half day spent in the factory. No child, young person or woman was to be allowed to eat in the dipping room, dippers' drying room or china-scouring room, and the factories were to be kept in a clean state, properly ventilated to prevent harm from dust 'or other Impurities generated in the Process of Manufacture that may be injurious to Health'.[25]

In 1865, Robert Baker, one of the inspectors, set out to 'render some of the most ruinous places untenable, and to induce the manufacturers to erect new buildings more suitable to their increasing demand for accommodation, and more in conformity with the progressive strides which the trade itself is making'. Such buildings, he believed, would necessarily involve 'improvements in architectural design, in trade machinery, in regulations, and in whatever could tend to relieve the earthenware manufacture of many of its present evils'. He recognised that there were obstacles to the immediate introduction of machinery:

> It requires, as it appears to me, a more educated class of workmen, a finer touch to regulate the speed, and a juster idea of the economy of power than as yet overspreads the minds of the potters generally. Moreover, it requires an outlay of which it will be difficult to impress the necessity on the minds of the masters; and last, and not least, it will require new buildings altogether in a majority of the 'Banks' to render its employment available and free from danger.[26]

However, the effects of investigation, outside interest and advice, and the co-operation of at least a number of the manufacturers, were felt immediately. This, combined with increasing foreign competition in pottery manufacture, stimulated a fresh attitude and phase of activity within the industry.

Able to consider and incorporate the new requirements at planning stage, the new factories displayed a quite immediate improvement in potwork architecture. It was especially evident in the installation of machinery and in the human concern shown for workers and facilities. Even in 1867 the inspector was reporting that such factories, with the best modern appliances, with the employment of machinery and the arrangement for carrying on all the divisions of labour with the least possible loss of either time or materials, 'must impress any visitor with the good effects that the enquiry into the potter's condition has accomplished already, and with the prospective advancement in the art of pottery which it promises'.[27]

The sudden withdrawal of unskilled labour following the implementation of a half-time education system, and the restriction on maximum hours, meant that the introduction of steam power quickly became an integral part of factory design. By 1871, the proportion of children under thirteen working in the potteries had dropped by half to 2,971.[28] In order to replace their unskilled labour in turning wheels, lathes, and jiggers, it was at last necessary to harness steam power to the 'making' shops, while fewer adult working hours made fully powered and improved production in the slip-making areas essential.

The *Staffordshire Advertiser* gave glowing accounts of the improvements. It was reported of the 1866 works of Anthony Shaw in Newport, Burslem, that:

> the orderly arrangement of the multifarious descriptions of rooms required, the light, and heat, and ventilation, the cleanliness and comfort, and the presence of mechanical appliances unknown until within the last few years, contrast most favourably with the straggling, disconnected, dark, dirty, and depressing sheds with which our forefathers were well-contented, but which are gradually giving way under the influence of modern capital and legislation and the recognition by employers of their duties towards their workpeople...[29]

The factory, designed even at this date by the manufacturer himself, was fully equipped for steam power and heating. It also had an improved

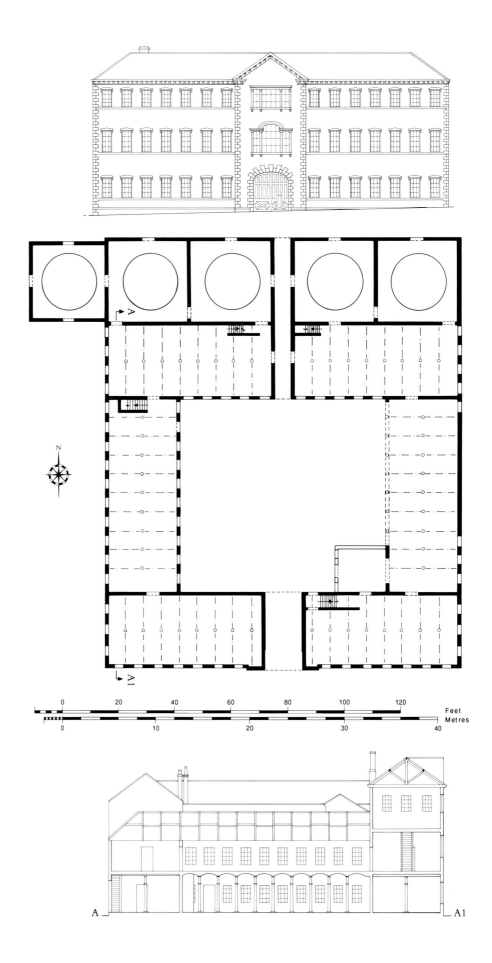

Figure 2
*Aynsley's Portland
Works, Longton*

2a *front elevation*

2b *ground-floor plan*

2c *section A–A1*

stove system, using revolving shelves within a small unit. It was still hot, but, at 95°F, an improvement on the earlier stoves. Also, as the reporter noted, the stove could be operated without all of the boy assistants needed in the old system. Finally, the works was lit by gas, and much of its ground was paved with blue brick or granite blocks. This was obviously something novel enough to warrant a mention, at a time when in many of the works 'the yards...are formed of ashes, and in consequence of the transit over them of heavy laden carts, there are deep ruts formed in them, which hold water after rain, into which the workers are liable to step in dark mornings, and so to remain with wet feet for the whole day'.[30]

Changes in potworks' design

The improvements and changes brought about by legislation took place within the traditional framework of the potworks, with conservatism as much in evidence as ever. The 1860s did see the emergence of the linear plan, however, which although not common is worth describing for the ideas behind it and for its partial adoption in later manufactories. Examples of both the conventional and linear plans from this date have been recorded.

John Aynsley's Portland Works, erected on Sutherland Road in Longton in 1861, was built to a conventional plan and typifies the combination of enlightenment and tradition evident in the new factories of the time (Figure 2). Up to the mid nineteenth century the land to the north of Sutherland Road had remained largely undeveloped, but the Longton estate owner, Heathcote, had begun selling off plots along the roadside. In a series of legal transactions with his former partner, Sampson Bridgwood, whose financial assistance had enabled the purchase, John Aynsley bought 2 acres (0.8 ha) of land on which to build his manufactory.[31] The front of the works was an elaboration of the familiar traditional style, with a symmetrical, pedimented arrangement combining Italianate and Georgian features on the three-storeyed frontage and publicly visible east side (Plates 54 and 55). Its elegance suggests the importance of the impression which Aynsley wanted to create as a producer of high-quality china, and although it does not differ significantly from others, the concentration of detail which comes from the relatively short street frontage has more impact than those stretching out in length.

In plan and arrangement, the factory is remarkably similar to earlier works, based around a quadrangle and laid out for production in the same way. However, the compact courtyard

factory conveys a sense of economy and efficiency not seen in more sprawling works, or in the cramped but erratic potworks of its time. Structurally it is interesting for its partly iron framework, with arched ground-floor ceiling. A similar structure can be seen at the St Mary's Works in Longton, of 1862. Changes had occurred in subtle but important ways. The workrooms were wider and of greater height. The width of the workrooms was 8 yards (7.3 m) compared with that of 6 yards (5.5 m) in Masons and the Foley, while the room height had increased from 8 or 9 feet (2.4 m or 2.8 m) to 10 and 12 feet

Plate 54
Aynsley's Portland Works, Longton, 1861

Plate 55
Entrance to The Portland Works

(3 m and 3.7 m). The sense of spaciousness was increased by slightly larger and more numerous windows. The Portland factory was the product of Aynsley's working life in different potworks, and his involvement in its design reflected his interest in the well-being of his workers, something which some other less successful workmen turned manufacturers could not afford to consider. 'I have been a workman', he told the government commissioner, 'and have experienced the evil of working in a badly-ventilated room; and in building these works it has been my ambition to have my rooms as convenient and well-ventilated as possible for my workpeople.'[32] He was also opposed to long working hours and to the employment of young children, although he recognised that some manufacturers needed their labour.

It was with the Minton Hollins tile factory in Stoke that the block linear plan appeared, as an alternative to the courtyard and as a rationalisation of old tile works.[33] The factory, demolished in 1987 except for its front range, is of interest both because of its linear plan and as an indication of the respectability and attention which the industry was beginning to receive amongst the architectural profession (Plates 56 and 57).

The scope of the tile industry had widened in the first half of the nineteenth century, with the development of decorative tile-making. The medieval skill of encaustic, or inlaid, tile-making was taken up as a commercial venture by Herbert Minton, and came into production at his factory in 1840. The popularity of the tiles was immediate, and marked the beginning of a world-wide fashion for decorative tiles in architecture. Minton worked closely with the architect A W N Pugin, producing copies of medieval tiles as well as those using Pugin's own design for the architect's many Gothic Revival churches built between 1835 and 1852.[34] Copeland and Garrett began producing encaustic tiles at an early stage, as later did T and R Boote at the Waterloo Works in Burslem, but it was the firm of Minton Hollins and Co which became famous for its range of tiles, and which established a purpose-built factory for the production of tiles in response to the increased demand for this product.

Michael Daintry Hollins embarked on this new factory in 1868 with the help of money provided by a split with his partner Colin Minton Campbell. There had been three factories producing Minton tiles in Stoke; Hollins's idea was to build a single large factory capable of handling extensive production as efficiently as possible. He bought a 7-acre (2.8-ha) site alongside Foulea Brook, and employed the Potteries' most prominent architect, Charles Lynam, to undertake the design of the factory. Because the land was low and liable to flooding, the whole area was first raised by 6 feet (1.8 m) with pottery waste.[35]

The finished factory was to be 'specially arranged for the rapid and economical manipulation of large quantities of material', comprising a succession of blocks 'so arranged that, commencing with the mill and terminating with the packing house, every part corresponds in order with the successive processes undergone in the production of tiles'.[36] The rear line of buildings comprised the mill, slip houses and preparation areas. Parallel to these were the tile-making workshops with clay storage cellars underneath, further forward were the decorating

Plate 56
Minton Hollins tile factory, Stoke-on-Trent

shops and ovens, and finally, in the line fronting the road, were the warehouses and packing house. Thus, while the old courtyard arrangement was suited to the production of a wide variety of wares, a single and simple type of ware, albeit with several forms and treatments, could be produced most efficiently with a flow strictly in one direction, and its buildings designed accordingly.

The front range (Figure 3a) displays the peak of concern for presentation and advertising. Of red brick with blue brick dressings, the exceptionally long two-storeyed façade has stone banding over ground and first-floor windows, inset with small coloured tiles, while decorative tile panels head each of the ground-floor windows and were used to announce the firm's name over the main entrance. The building served the usual four functions: it accommodated packing and warehousing, offices and boardroom; acted as bridge between the factory and outside world, as main entrance to the site; and it held the showrooms and small museum which were its direct link with the public.

The inside and outside of this building alone were full of contrasts. At the centre were a magnificent hall, stairwell and landing, with showroom and museum on the ground floor, and offices upstairs. The whole was beautifully decorated with Minton Hollins tiles, whose impact is conveyed by a visitor to the works in 1878:

Plate 57
Entrance to Minton Hollins tile factory

Figure 3
Minton Hollins tile factory, Stoke-on-Trent

3a front elevation

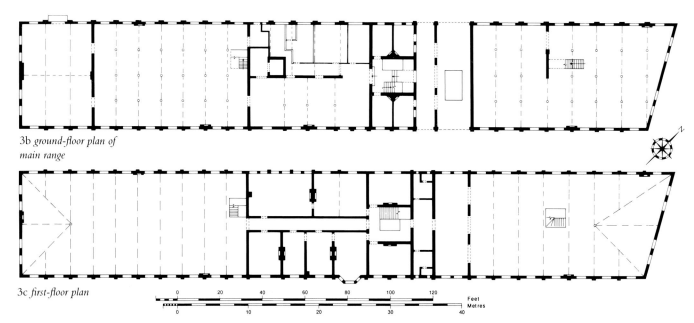

3b ground-floor plan of main range

3c first-floor plan

Feet
Metres

Figure 3
Minton Hollins tile factory, Stoke-on-Trent

Ascending the stairs that lead to corridor on corridor of offices, you see the walls covered with tiles of many designs, but all bearing as the central ornament the monogram of the firm. In every passage, they are still before you, and the floor on which you tread is inlaid with some of those famous encaustic tiles which…remind one of the world-wide reknown [sic] which their manufacturer has achieved…[37]

The windows in the central area had large panes, the main office an oriel window, and the central corridor upstairs was enhanced by skylighting. Consideration was given to uniformity at the front of the range, while at the rear, seen only by the employees, window-spacing was subordinated to the provision of maximum lighting in the central area, especially in the boardroom. The warehousing and packing rooms in the block were huge unplastered shells supported by iron columns, with the steel girder framework exposed. The large showroom shared this structure, but the walls were plastered, the columns ornamented and the girders boxed in. The building had a central boiler and pipe system, and also fireplaces: those in the administrative rooms were ornate and tiled, those elsewhere were plain, functional openings in the chimney-breasts.

Behind the façade, the works was without relief or ornament. The long open rooms in the surviving workshop range show that the limited number of techniques and types of ware needed few room divisions. The ground floor (Figure 3b) was used for the manufacture of pressed tiles and mosaics, the upper floor (Figure 3c) for encaustic tiles. The third floor (Figure 3d) was probably used as a mould store. The building was nevertheless not without inconveniences: it appears, for instance, to have had only one staircase (which was internal), to which all movement of people and materials was directed. To some extent this was alleviated by trapdoors (which were also used in the warehousing areas), used to pass moulds and ware from one floor to another.

The plan chosen by Michael Daintry Hollins was particularly suited to tile manufacture, but it was also adopted by the earthenware manufacturers Cartwright and Edwards for the Borough Pottery, along Trentham Road in Longton, in 1869, a works described as a model for its time.[38] This appears to be an isolated case, however, and within the industry as a whole, the traditional courtyard plan maintained its hold.

BRICK AND TILE MANUFACTURING

While the revival of the manufacture of fine tiles had become an important venture within the main pottery industry, the old-established brick and tile manufacturing had also expanded, to satisfy the demand for building materials which had been generated by the growing urban community. Manufacturing occurred primarily in a geographical band sweeping down from Tunstall along the west of the Potteries, to Trent Vale and Hanford, coinciding with an extensive bed of red marl. Unlike domestic pottery-making, the manufacture of bricks was still carried out using local clay and marl. The availability of clay as well as coal remained a vital factor in siting, and the brick-works were set up directly along the clay beds.

The 'making' process was a simple one. In the early years of the nineteenth century, both bricks and tiles were still made individually, by throwing a lump of soft clay into a mould and cutting off the excess with a wire bow. Clay was dug, brought into the mill to be ground and mixed, and then taken directly to the 'making' sheds for moulding. The unfired bricks were dried outside, in open sheds, or later, in sheds with flues running along the centre of the building. The dried bricks were then taken to the kiln to be fired. The manufacturing process involved none of the complexities of planning or design required by the pottery industry, and the works remained simple. There was only one 'making' process, no cross-movement, no decoration, and only one firing; and so there was no need for any connecting buildings on the sites. On maps, the ovens are either shown dotted around the site or are not identifiable. In 1850 it was suggested that the brickmaker owning his works might occupy around 6 acres (2.4 ha), have a five-horsepower steam engine, a set of horizontal rollers, a pug-mill, six oblong drying houses and nine ovens. The smaller manufacturer renting his premises might have only one moulding and drying house, a pug-mill, and 'a breadth of brick floor and marl bank sufficient to work one oven'.[39]

The second half of the century was a period of change, with expansion and the introduction of more mechanisation. Despite the many patents which had been taken out in the first half of the century, it was said to be the withdrawal of excise duty on bricks in 1850 which had generated the serious investigation and adoption of mechanical processes. The design of manufactories themselves correspondingly began to receive attention. In 1856 Humphrey Chamberlain, a draining engineer, described the best arrangement as being a compact, single building enterprise:

The whole works should be under one roof, and only occupy a fraction of the space devoted to this manufacture in the field. The brick manufactory may be a square construction, a fourth of which, across the top, would be occupied by the steam power mills and machines, with an allowance for working room; one half would be used for during [hardening] the ware, and the remaining quarter for kiln room.[40]

How far the Potteries manufacturers adopted the new design ideas appears to have varied in the same way that it did in the lighter clay industry. The 1878 Ordnance Survey maps show a variety of plans, some composed of scattered groupings, some of semi-courtyard groups, others of single-structure layouts. The Wheatley brick and tiles works, built on the side of the Newcastle road at Trent Vale around 1870, consisted of a spread of

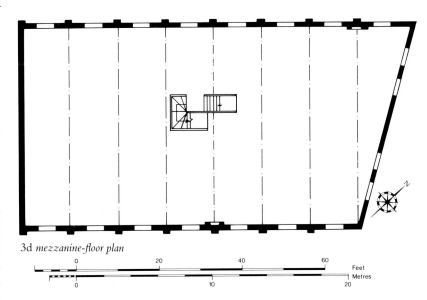

3d *mezzanine-floor plan*

Feet
Metres

Figure 3
Minton Hollins tile factory, Stoke-on-Trent

disconnected buildings.[41] The steam-powered grinding mill is at the back of the premises on the edge of the clay pit. 'Making' and drying took place in the same sheds, some single and some two-storeyed. These had a system of heating flues running beneath the ground floor. A coal heap lay outside the end of each shed or group of sheds to feed the fire at the opening there, and it was one man's job to go around tending each fire. The sheds were very low, for economy of heat, and one of those surviving has no windows, giving a dungeon-like atmosphere. In one of its bays a hand-pressing tile machine, which was operated by a man and a boy assistant, still stands. According to a former worker at the factory, this was the only machine in the shed, and the other bays were used for stacking the tiles to dry when removed from the central flue area.[42] From here the tiles were taken in barrows to the kilns outside each shed. The 'making' areas were divided: in the long two-storeyed range which was in line with the sheds, quarry tiles were made on the ground floor, shaped and ridge tiles above. The factory had its own fitter's, joiner's and blacksmith's shop, for making dies and moulds.

GRINDING MILLS

With the overall expansion of the pottery industry, ancillary trades and industries also grew and prospered. The number of grinding mills in the Potteries operating for public use had increased to twenty-five by 1851.[43] Some of these were owned by manufacturers and erected on or near to their factory sites, while the rest were owned and run independently. Two of the latter, the Furlong Mill in Burslem (1843) and Shirley's

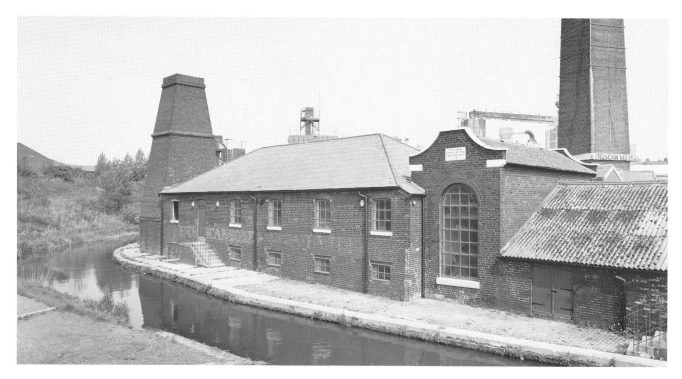

Plate 58
Shirley's Etruscan Bone and Flint Mill by the Trent and Mersey Canal at Etruria Lock

Plate 59
Shirley's Etruscan Bone and Flint Mill: the shaft room

Etruscan Bone and Flint Mill in Etruria (1856), are still operating today. Both were steam-powered and both were situated by the canal, the raw materials being brought down from Liverpool by barge.

The Furlong Mill has been entirely converted inside for modern production, though it continues to use traditional kilns and firing methods. The Etruscan Mill is still owned and run by the Shirley family, and while half of the premises have been rebuilt for present-day working, the original grinding mill has been preserved intact and leased by the family to the Stoke-on-Trent City Museum and Art Gallery. It has been fully restored and is open to the public.

The Etruscan Bone and Flint Mill

The Etruscan Bone and Flint Mill (Plate 58) is situated on its own canal arm between the Trent and Mersey Canal and the Caldon Canal, immediately below their junction at Etruria. The site was formerly occupied by a firm which boiled and calcined bone, which was then taken for grinding at the nearby Bell's Mill. One of the partners, John Bourne, bought the site in 1842, and when he died, ten years later, he left a quarter of his estate to the brothers Jesse and Joseph Shirley. In 1856 construction began on the Etruscan Mill by George Kirk, a prominent local builder who specialised in mills.[44]

Kirk designed a compact, logical arrangement on the irregular site. There were two points of access, one from the canal, the other at the far end fronting the road to Etruria and Shelton. At that end were the lodgekeeper's cottage and office, with weighing-machine outside and a small round pond for water on the further side. Along the northern boundary of the site were the single-storey sheds for storing materials, convenient for access from both the canal – where there was a crane for lifting the materials from the barges – and the road. The milling process took place in the two main buildings on site: grinding in the block fronting the canal, and drying on raised beds in the building behind it. Only the first building survives, and that has been partially demolished at the rear to make way for modern buildings belonging to the present mill. Nevertheless, it is the most important structure and, complete with

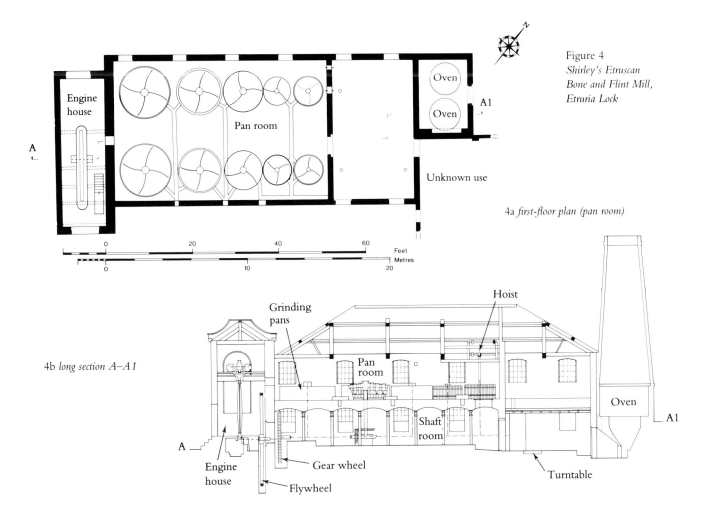

Figure 4
Shirley's Etruscan Bone and Flint Mill, Etruria Lock

4a *first-floor plan (pan room)*

4b *long section A–A1*

its machinery and steam engine, provides a perfect model of its era.

The low, mainly two-storeyed building extends along the east side of the canal with just enough space outside for loading and unloading materials. At one end are the two calcining ovens, which share a single rectangular hovel structure. From here the flint and bone passed through to a crusher room, entered externally by steps down to the semi-basement level. At present, a small steam engine operates a jaw crusher in this room, both of which were installed at a later date. Beyond this room was the large shaft room, containing two line shafts with bevelled gear drives to operate the grinding pans in the room above. The shaft room had fire-proof iron columns and a brick-arched ceiling structure which helped bear the load of the pan room and its heavy equipment (Plate 59). The calcined material was lifted through a hatchway to the pan room by a 2-ton capacity hoist. A turntable in the crusher room by the entrance to the shaft room was used to manoeuvre a loaded kibble or truck of material through the doorway and under the hatch, ready to be lifted.

The pan room (Figure 4) was entered at first-floor level by an external staircase. It originally accommodated twelve grinding pans of varying size, the largest, of iron, 12 feet (3.6 m) in diameter, the smallest, wooden, ones 6 feet (1.8 m) in diameter (Plate 60). In each pan were three or four curved arms attached to a central vertical

Plate 60
Shirley's Etruscan Bone and Flint Mill: the pan room

Plate 61
Shirley's Etruscan Bone and Flint Mill: the engine house

shaft. The floor of the pans was made up of Flintshire chert blocks, the gaps being filled with broken biscuit ware. The bone and flint were crushed by chert stones pushed round the pans by the rotating arms. A hand-operated crane at the

end of the room near to the four largest pans was used to help lift these runner stones when they needed adjusting or replacing. The flint and bone were ground in water, and at the end of eight hours' grinding the pan outlets were opened to

allow the slurry to flow out along channels in the floor, to holes where it fell into wooden conduits suspended from the shaft room ceiling. From there it was directed into the washtubs, where any coagulated particles were separated by stirring with paddles. The slurry was then passed through a sieve, and from there pumped to settling tanks, where the clear water was gradually drained off until the desired consistency was achieved.

Next door to the main mill building is the engine house, and then the boiler house, the two set back slightly from the rest. The engine house is a narrow, single-storeyed room, purpose-built to accommodate the beam engine with its iron wheel 20 feet (6.1 m) in diameter (Plate 61). Open steps lead along the side up to the beam itself on the upper platform level. The present engine, which was installed by George Kirk during the mill's construction in 1856–7, is said to have been built by J and T Sherratt during the 1830s, and may have been used initially in a Lancashire cotton mill. The original boiler was replaced in 1953. Water was fed to the boiler from an iron tank in the boiler-house roof, possibly pumped through by a beam-operated pump. A pipe from the boiler passed steam through the wall to the engine next door.

Inside, the mill is arranged and fitted with consideration for each piece of equipment and each part of the process, and for the smooth running of the whole. Externally, the different areas were also treated in what was thought to be an appropriate manner. The main building displays modest, purely functional features. The shaft room has a series of small, shallow windows barely sufficient to light the room, while on the upper storey there are larger sash windows to the main working room, the pan room. Just as the steam engine formed the heart of the mill and its source of pride, so the frontage of the engine house was treated accordingly. It has the only decorative façade, with sculpted pediment hiding the roof line and complete with date and name panel inset in the brickwork. The high, arched window (that of the classic textile-mill engine house) extends from ground to first-floor level; its design not only allowed the engine to be more easily conveyed into the building, but also provided the focal point of the mill through which could be seen its showpiece, the engine and its impressive wheel. In contrast to this section of the mill, the boiler house alongside is the most basic and simple structure on the site, a low building with no windows and only a pair of plain wooden doors.

Aside from its attractiveness in situation and design, it is the pure and perfect functionalism of

the mill which impresses, though it is a functionalism concerned with technology and materials rather than with the human workforce. Even now that the working rooms have been cleaned, it is still possible to imagine the enormous injury to health caused by the flint and bone dust, with no provision to alleviate the problem, and with no facilities for workers for anything other than work. This particular branch of the industry was as dangerous as any other, and its buildings contributed to the risks.

Plate 62
190 Waterloo Road, Cobridge, an area between Burslem and Hanley that attracted superior housing as the town centres became cramped

THE GROWTH OF MIDDLE-CLASS HOUSING

During the second half of the century, the manufacturers had gradually been moving out of the town centres to new areas on the fringes of the existing communities. Waterloo Road, built in 1817 and extending from Burslem to Hanley, attracted superior dwellings, built not only along the line of the road but eventually in the whole area of Bleak Hill and Cobridge as well. Several of these houses remain, in what has become a much neglected part of the City. One of the best preserved, 190 Waterloo Road, was built around 1830 (Plate 62). Standing in a row of three similar detached early Victorian houses, it is a large, square dwelling built of yellow brick with stone quoins and a low, hipped tiled roof. There are large bay windows on the ground floor, while on the first floor are three evenly spaced windows with stone surrounds and labelled stone lintels. The front entrance has an elegant columned stone

Plate 63
21 The Villas, London Road, Stoke-on-Trent. The Villas was developed by the Stokeville Building Society between 1851 and 1855

portico. The whole is set back from the road on a raised bank, with steps leading up to the front, a front garden bounded by a low stone wall, and spacious and secluded gardens to the rear. The spirit of past pride and status is perhaps more easily recaptured in these few houses along Waterloo Road than anywhere else in the Potteries.

By the middle of the century the area of Northwood, to the north of Hanley, was becoming a retreat of the middle classes, as was Stoke Road leading from Shelton to Stoke, and, a little later in the 1860s, the new suburbs of Dresden and Florence, south of Longton. The most distinctive and isolated group of houses built for the middle classes – 'The Villas', erected by the Stokeville Building Society between 1851 and 1855 – included pottery manufacturers and the élite of artists amongst its tenants. The Society was formed by a number of prominent local inhabitants in order to provide the means for its membership to erect and own houses on copyhold land at what became known as 'Stokeville',

outside the town centre. The leading Potteries architect Charles Lynam was employed to design three classes of house for the scheme, amounting to twenty-four houses. The Italianate villa style (Plate 63) which Lynam adopted was more fully developed here than anywhere else in the Potteries.[45]

The Villas was set back from the main road, so that the houses enjoyed both privacy and seclusion, and faced on to a private service road. Each house stood on its own generous plot of land, which was used for the laying out of ordered gardens. As one of the first class, Number 14 was at the end farthest from the public road, on high ground. It has features typical of the villa design: the asymmetrical composition, the pan-tiled, low pitched roof, the stucco wall finish, the inclusion of a tower as an integral part of the house, and windows and doors with heavy moulded surrounds. The two more public sides of the house were the main focus of attention, while the rear and northern sides were far more subdued.

The first-class villa comprised four main bedrooms, each with a fireplace, and a further room, presumably that of the servants, on the second floor in the tower, reached by a discreet staircase. The master bedroom at the front of the house had an adjoining dressing room. A bathroom was situated in between the two rear bedrooms, and a separate water-closet off the landing near to the main staircase. Only the bathroom had a window (which was of stained glass) overlooking the service area at the rear of the premises; the two back bedrooms were given windows on to the sides of the house.

On the ground floor, the Victorian preoccupation with privacy and segregation was visible to an even greater extent. The front entrance opened on to a hall, on either side of which were the drawing-room and dining-room. At the back of the house was the breakfast-room, and beside it the kitchen. The kitchen and the washroom (which was set back slightly from the rest of the house) were a relatively independent section, and the rear tradesmen's entrance was situated there. The division between the private and service areas on the ground floor is distinctly marked by the change in quality of the floor tiles. Those in the main hall are coloured encaustic tiles, laid in a star pattern, while those in the passage adjoining the kitchen door and tradesmen's entrance are relatively plain red tiles.

Leading from the breakfast-room at the rear of the house was a long rectangular conservatory, which had a brick wall on the side nearest to the yard hiding the service area from the gardens. At right angles to this, a row of outbuildings formed an additional side to the courtyard, while behind the yard itself were the coach-house and stables, which opened directly on to the road at the rear of the premises. Beside them was the general rear entrance.

The social range of the pottery manufacturers had broadened – many new to the industry were of very moderate means compared with the old-established potters. This was especially the case in Longton, where the majority of works were of small and medium size. Accordingly, not all owners were able to afford the luxuries of a large and impressive villa. On a more modest, but still comfortable, scale, were the many smaller, semi-detached or terraced properties built for the manufacturers and their associates. Falling into this category were some of the houses erected in the Duke of Sutherland's scheme in the Dresden and Florence suburbs during the 1860s. Numbers 62 and 64 Trentham Road, Florence, were built in 1865–6.[46] They are typical of the Duke's Trentham Estate style of ornate Gothic Revival,

Plate 64
62 and 64 Trentham Road, Florence, Longton

but include *palazzo*-style Italianate windows on the first floor (Plate 64). They were built of yellow and red brick, used to decorative effect, with slate roofs. The two houses reflected social divisions just as their superiors did. The kitchen, washroom, pantry and cellar were self-contained, the domain of the servants only, and there was a separate outside access for tradesmen and servants. Upstairs were three bedrooms and a bathroom – the existence of the latter in itself showing the houses' innovation and superiority – while a second set of stairs led up to a servants' room.

The Villas and other housing groups of the period show clearly that in whatever ways the pottery industry and its architecture might be a peculiarly local feature, the homes of its owners and managers were those of the Victorian middle classes everywhere, reflecting similar interests, aspirations and social mores.

WORKING-CLASS HOUSING

Meanwhile, most of the population remained in the town centres. Not all of the more affluent had moved away, but by far the worst-off were the poorer, working families living in the small terraced streets and back alleys. By 1850 the population had risen to over 86,000 and the town centres had become packed with small groups of housing amongst the potworks.[47] When the government commissioner, Robert Stanley, carried out his inquiries in 1845, it was found that the Potteries were not the worst in terms of living conditions, for they were 'built in an irregular and rather dispersed manner, on moderate declivities affording a good fall of water', and at least had some spaces around the houses, areas of unoccupied land, and some 'tolerably wide and open' main streets.[48] In Tunstall, especially, the standard of housing compared favourably with other towns. Nevertheless, there was appalling squalor in certain areas of the six towns. The mortality rate of between twenty-four and twenty-eight per thousand was average for industrial towns but far above the national average of eighteen.[49] The primary cause of the poor conditions was the absence of a sanitary and drainage system and of any sense of responsibility for providing one, together with a lack of control over housing developments. The situation was worst where the general absence of sanitary and sewage provision was combined with the oldest and densest areas of housing, and dwellings with no through ventilation.

The main health hazard came not only in the planned courts but in those which had been formed almost accidentally, with houses wedged in against others as part of the infill of the town centres. There is no evidence of there ever having been more than a small number of planned back-to-back houses in the Potteries, despite official reports suggesting that this had once been the case.[50] While they should not be compared with the large, infamous blocks of back-to-backs elsewhere, the many single dwellings tagged on to others, squeezed into nooks and crannies, nonetheless had a similar effect of preventing air flow through and around the houses. In many cases, houses were built up against pottery factories, so that not only was the toxicity of air increased, but also household and industrial waste was mingled in the back alleys and confined spaces of the town centres.

Design faults in the houses too were centred on ventilation with the 'perverse habit [which] seems to have been established of constructing the windows in such a manner as that they cannot be opened at all, or only to a very small extent'. In some houses 'there are no back windows at all, in fact, no back opening of any kind. In the top rooms also there is often no fireplace or flue, or if there be one, the opening is carefully pasted up with paper, or otherwise closed effectually.' Such faults were aggravated by families blocking up any ventilation points in an effort to keep warm. In some cases the reverse happened, when frustrated tenants broke holes in the fixed windows 'stuffing the opening this made with rags, which they occasionally remove to admit a little air'.[51]

Improvements in workers' housing

Just as government inquiries, investigations and legislation were to stimulate improvements in the pottery industry and its architecture, so they heralded a new phase in workers' housing. There was an atmosphere of change in the Potteries as elsewhere, though any immediate and far-reaching changes in workers' housing and conditions were unlikely, especially in the face of hostility from influential property-owners. The 1841 Royal Commission on sewage, sanitation and water supply, while not directly concerned with housing as such, educated public opinion on the whole issue and brought the misery of working-class living conditions to everyone's attention. A number of improvements were to take place in the Potteries in the light of the contemporary social climate and of government legislation, and they proved to be a logical progression in the design of workers' housing. There were two main influences on change. One was the establishment of the local boards of health and the introduction of housing by-laws; the other was the part played by the freehold land societies and by individuals who took the initiative in improvements even before the local boards had made any impact.[52]

As the nineteenth century progressed, both the housing and labour markets expanded, whilst the practice of supplying workers' houses declined amongst many employers, especially those with smaller enterprises. Many manufacturers inherited existing houses, and they also tended to rely on the stock of housing built by other agencies because it was much easier and cheaper to do this than to build improved dwellings for their workers themselves. Some of the major manufacturers and colliery proprietors undertook new developments, either for reasons of prestige in the form of small groups of model housing, or more generally to cater for the new housing demand which they had created in areas outside the existing town centres, or simply as a speculative venture. New initiatives were on the whole slow and uninspired, but some made a notable impact and contribution to the scene. The mixture of old and new, of model and basic housing, meant a very wide range in the standard of dwellings.

Several features identify the housing developments of this period. Firstly, developments were much larger than before, in some cases consisting of a hundred or more houses. Secondly, they were laid out in a grid pattern in accordance with new regulations regarding street width, spacing and ventilation. The back alley and passage between pairs of houses became the standard requirement to provide access and ventilation. Thirdly, local society was at its most fully developed and there were sufficient people within each level to result in housing estates comprising a number of different grades. Finally, the new estates were situated outside the cramped existing centres, either in pockets of open space between the towns or beyond them on the fringes of the built-up area.

The houses themselves are equally distinctive. From the 1850s the modern house was extended yet again at the rear, to give a back kitchen or wash-house and in some cases a third bedroom above. The extension was a narrow one, built across only one part of the house so that light could still be provided in the existing back room. The water-closet was introduced as an integral part of the house or else an individual privy was provided in the backyard of each. The water-closet and the coal-shed were attached to the end of the wash-house. The paramount importance placed on space and ventilation found expression in a minimum size of rooms, ceiling heights of 9 feet (2.7 m) and windows which could be opened at least halfway. Taller windows (with the eventual introduction of the bay window in the best houses), large panes of glass and the fanlight over the front door all allowed in more light. Warmth was ensured by the provision of fireplaces in every room.

These new features were reflections not only of contemporary concern for health and sanitation but of the same social preoccupations that were to be found in superior housing. Downstairs, space was quite strictly divided into parlour, kitchen, pantry under the often centrally situated staircase, and the wash-house, coal-shed and water-closet at the rear. The hall was introduced into the superior house, so that entrance was no longer directly into the front parlour. In practice, the parlour became the 'best' room in imitation of the middle classes, reserved for special occasions and for visitors. As one historian has put it, it represented 'a triumph over poverty and challenge to the external environment which was too often one of dirt, squalor and social disharmony'.[53] Upstairs, three bedrooms were erected either by building over the back kitchen, or by making use of the space over the outside passage. The three rooms not only allowed the parents to sleep separately from the children, but also the children of each sex to have their own room.

Outside there were two points of interest. One was that the garden returned as an attribute of the better-class worker's home, offering the family the privilege of space and a more pleasant outlook, as well as the opportunity to grow vegetables once more. The other noticeable feature was a burgeoning of decorative features on the façade of the house, borrowed from houses of superior status, and a more adventurous use of building materials.

The materials used varied according to the grades of workers' housing. The basic house was of red brick and tiles, and if there was any relief it was in plain brick dentilling. Coinciding with the popularity of yellow brick in middle-class housing, some groups were built in that distinctive colour, while yellow and blue brick were occasionally used in decorative form on red brick houses. The only houses known to have been built entirely of blue brick are the railway cottages at Fenton.[54] The popular trend for using ceramic tiles in architecture during the second half of the nineteenth century was also reflected in the superior terraced house. Inside, red and blue quarry tiles created patterns in entrance halls, with the plain red tiles in the kitchen. Outside, tiled panels were used as ornament.

Many more houses from the second half of the century survive than from the earlier period, though those that have been surveyed tend to be also of particular interest and merit rather than representative of the most basic speculative housing. It is these houses and others like them, however, which are the more important landmarks in the Potteries; they set the standards for others to follow.

'Model' housing: Hartshill

The nearest that any mid nineteenth-century Potteries' manufacturer came to the erecting of a model village was the development undertaken by Herbert Minton at Hartshill. The Granville Estate, built at Cobridge in 1853 by iron and coal-master Earl Granville, was a much larger and more ambitious project in mass workers' housing, but the Minton development was more impressive architecturally, and reflected the gentlemanly concept of workers' housing which prevailed in the middle of the century.[55]

Minton himself already lived in a 'very beautiful and compact cottage residence' in Hartshill, elevated above the smoke of his Stoke manufactories and in an area with only a scattering of cottages.[56] By planning his village he was making a community entirely his own, without the inconvenience of being surrounded by mass housing or industrial buildings. The development was planned on the Stoke side of his own house, and was centred on a new church and vicarage, built in 1841–2, and school, built in 1852. In 1857, a little further down on the other side of the road, he built a row of ten cottages, to which his nephew was later to add more dwellings in the

Plate 65
*Minton Cottages,
Hartshill*

Plate 66
Hartshill Institute

same style (Plate 65) and a mechanics' institute (Plate 66).[57] This was a personal venture affecting his own home environment and offering the opportunity to enhance and advertise his status. It is not surprising, therefore, that Minton engaged one of the country's leading architects, George Gilbert Scott, to carry out the work and chose an elaborate Gothic style, which not only achieved harmony between the church (Plate 67) and other buildings but also had the greatest architectural impact.[58]

It seems likely that Scott designed the cottages as well as the church, vicarage and school. He had already designed a much larger development of housing for Edward Ackroyd at Ackroyden in Yorkshire, in 1855.[59] The Minton cottages,

probably as a result of Herbert Minton's personal attention, represented a considerable improvement in workers' accommodation in the Potteries.

The cottage development was designed as a row of eight terraced dwellings with a detached house standing at each end. Positioned so as to overlook the valley between Hartshill and Hanley, they were set back from the road with long banked gardens at the rear. Their location was an enviable one: those living there were within walking distance of Stoke and their place of employment, but well out of the smoke and grime which their fellow workers had to endure. In 1856, when the cottages were being planned, a reporter from the local newspaper wrote: 'We hear that Mr. Minton is...about to erect eight dwelling houses at Hartshill. Truely, this liberality is great.'[60] It was great to the extent of erecting houses of a very superior quality, but not in terms of providing them for any significant number of his employees, for this was a token group for a select number of workers – those who were either the more highly paid or the longest-serving employees, or both. Moreover, even within this small group of houses, distinct classes were displayed. In the detached houses in 1861 lived a cashier and the manager of the tile works. In one of the end terraces was the widow of Minton's bailiff, in the other a woman receiving an annuity. The other six cottages were occupied by two warehousemen, an overman, a slip-maker, a modeller and a foreman, all of whom were respected workers of comparatively long service and valued by Minton as faithful servants.[61]

At the time, there was talk of the cottages being almshouses, for which the Elizabethan

Gothic style was considered appropriate. While not all of the occupants were Minton's 'aged workmen', the number of older employees amongst them was sufficient to make this a probable consideration in his scheme.[62]

The cottages were highly ornate. The six central ones each had a steeply pitched roof, with patterned tiles and decorative ridge tiles, topped by a tall chimney. They were of red brick with four levels of blue brick banding. The main upper-floor window had a dormer roof with patterned tile inset, elaborate surround and bracketed sill, the small window had honeycomb-patterned panes of glass. The ground-floor casement window had a brick-arched lintel and mosaic tile panel. Each house shared a gabled double porch, with tiled inset and barge boards, and a pointed Gothic front door. A sign of the quality of the dwellings is that the rear of the buildings show equal attention to detail, with flared double brick lintels, stone sills, Gothic-style window frames and, upstairs, leaded lights.

Inside, the cottages were well laid out, with up-to-date facilities. Each had three bedrooms, one 13 feet by 11 feet (3.9 m by 3.4 m), one 12 feet by 9 feet (3.6 m by 2.7 m) and the other small room 7 feet 6 inches by 6 feet (2.3 m by 1.8 m). In the rear bedroom there was a fitted cupboard over the stairs. Downstairs, an entrance hall led to the front parlour, which was 12 feet wide (3.6 m), and the back room, 12 feet 6 inches by 11 feet (3.8 m by 3.4 m), behind which were the wash-house, 10 feet 6 inches by 6 feet 6 inches (3.2 m x 2 m), a coal-shed and a privy. Each cottage had a cellar below.

The end cottages were even more elaborate: each had a bay window in the front parlour and its own side porch. They were very slightly larger, but had similar facilities inside except that there were two large bedrooms instead of three smaller ones.

CONCLUSION

In general, the earlier lack of discrimination between classes of building had been replaced by much greater concern with separation and with environment. To an extent, superior housing developments were isolated from both workers' housing and the factories. Some developments from the 1860s, however, such as the one at Dresden, included several classes of housing, from terraced streets to detached villas. In this respect the residential became separated from the industrial and commercial, or any other undesirable premises. Increasingly, stipulations were laid down in conditions of sale to this effect:

in 1866, for example, the executors of the Methodist manufacturer John Ridgway's estate at Shelton, offered plots for sale on the condition that they be used for 'no tavern, hostel, spirit vaults, ale house, beer house, dancing saloon, music hall, common lodging house or slaughterhouse...or any noisome manufactory or trade'.[63] Moreover, where possible, care was taken to build away from the smoke so that the more fortunate inhabitants at least could enjoy a cleaner atmosphere.

By the final quarter of the nineteenth century there was an air of improvement both in the pottery industry and in local housing. The new factories offered better working conditions for their employees. Housing standards had been raised, and the urban environment was at last being considered. Even in an ideal situation, however, the task of improvement would have taken effort and time, because of the sheer volume of work to be done (Plate 68). As it was, there were many kinds of obstacles to progress. Manufacturers were uncooperative, through lack of finance, constraints on their premises, or indifference. Landlords had no interest in improving their houses, nor speculative builders in providing anything other than the bare minimum in terms of standard and quality of housing. The local boards of health were hampered by their own apathy and by individual interests: property-owners, rate-payers and even the working families (who were threatened with the loss of the pigs in their backyards, an important supplement to their living). The way forward, as in all industrial towns, would be gradual and hesitant.

Plate 67
*Holy Trinity Church,
Hartshill, designed by
George Gilbert Scott*

Chapter 5

THE LATER NINETEENTH CENTURY: ECONOMY AND RENEWAL

Price's works was small, old-fashioned, and out of repair — one of those properties which are forlorn from the beginning, which bring despair into the hearts of a succession of owners, and which, being ultimately deserted, seem to stand forever in pitiable ruin. The arched entrance for carts into the yard was at the top of the steepest rise of the street, when it might as well have been at the bottom; and this was but one example of the architect's fine disregard for the principle of economy working — that principle to which in the scheming of manufacturies everything else is now so strictly subordinated...

Bennett 1902

From the mid 1870s, the Potteries' prosperity declined as international competition took its toll. Pottery exports reached their peak value in 1873, while in the last three decades of the century the value of imports increased many times over to £743,000.[1] Faced with such competition, the manufacturers could not raise their prices, and they were forced instead to look at cheaper production. Attempts to achieve this by reducing wages were largely unsuccessful, and so the alternative, introducing machinery to speed up production and save labour, was increasingly adopted.

It was not an easy solution. Cramped layouts and disconnected workshops made difficult the introduction of line-shafting for steam-powered potters' machines, and the smaller manufacturers had not the money either for machinery or for remodelling their premises. There were many potworks like that of Bates, Hall and Co at Dale Hall, which was said to bring to mind 'a big overgrown boy, who has become too big for his trousers, and has been compelled to have a patch on here and a lengthening out there'.[2] New and old co-existed in individual factories, both architecturally and in production methods. Alteration and partial rebuilding at the Hughes's family manufactory at Bournes Bank, Burslem, in 1876 meant that 'the front, a well-built and arranged structure, fitted up with every new style of machinery, reveals the science of today; while the premises in the rear look back to the time when this art was much less advanced'.[3] In the same vein, in 1886 a US Consul, based in Germany but on a visit to England, observed of the town of Tunstall:

> *Even the machinery and working methods employed, show the gradual development [of the factories]. Improvements and new appliances, while rapidly introduced now, do not at once displace all old tools. While some remind us of the time of the Pharaohs, others in the same factory bear the stamp of the greatest era of invention and are models of ingenuity. One still sees in the same factory with steam and other appliances of the most improved pattern, boys turning the wheel for the potter.[4]*

Engineering firms had become an important adjunct to the pottery industry, but the nature of the old buildings in which their machinery would have to operate meant that to a large extent they were still designing hand-operated equipment. Even in the early years of the present century, William Boulton was producing new machinery which could be operated either by hand or by steam power, and which therefore might be adopted in all but the most unsatisfactory premises.[5]

Plate 68
Marl Hole, Daisy Bank, Longton (photograph taken 1875). The juxtaposition of housing and potworks, in this case on the edge of a marl pit and shard tip, was a familiar scene in the nineteenth-century Potteries

In some potworks, steam power was introduced into the preparation area of the premises only. An example of this is to be found in the Gladstone Pottery Museum in Longton, a museum created out of a mid nineteenth-century factory to provide an understanding of early industrial pottery-making. The museum captures perfectly the courtyard arrangement of the potworks, with small workshops surrounding the cobbled yard, the latter dominated by two bottle ovens (Plate 69). This, as in other factories, was added to piecemeal, and towards the end of the

Plate 69
Courtyard of the Gladstone Pottery, Longton (now the Gladstone Pottery Museum)

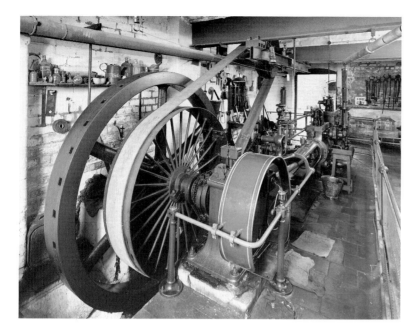

Plate 70
Steam engine at the Gladstone Pottery

century an engine house was built in the yard. The ground floor of the engine house survives, with steam engine (not original), which was used to power the adjoining slip-preparation room (Plate 70). The whole sequence of mixing and sieving can still be seen here, not only enabling an understanding of the process but also an appreciation of the efficiency of the arrangement and the modest sophistication which it brought to an otherwise handcraft-based potworks. In this

respect as in others, the Gladstone must be typical of the many medium-sized factories occupied in the second half of the last century.

CONSOLIDATION OF THE INDUSTRY

Nevertheless, while many manufacturers continued to struggle within the confines of existing premises, fresh activity in factory-building was taking place, now no longer in the immediate wake of the Factory Acts of the 1860s, but reflecting the consolidation and maturing of a century of industrial experience. Large new factories were being built by well-established and thriving firms, astute enough to find the choice plots of land which were still in evidence near the central areas. The main influence on location was even more firmly a site's convenience for transport and communications. Winkle and Co, who had been operating in Hanley, moved out to their new Colonial factory in Whieldon Road, Stoke, in 1889, on a site offering 'exceptional facilities on account of its proximity to the canal and railway'. Porcelain manufacturers Boulton and Floyd outgrew their premises at Cliffe Bank and moved to Lovatt and Hall Street in Stoke, to a factory built to their own design. Thomas Twyford already had the Bath Street Works in Hanley, when in 1879 he built his works at Cliffe Vale for the production of sanitary ware. It was ideally situated, with the canal along its northern

Plate 71
Twyford's sanitary ware factory, 1879, designed by Robert Scrivener and built alongside the canal and road at Cliffe Vale

Caradon Twyfords

side, railway sidings constructed on the other, and a main road to the front (Plates 71 and 72).[6]

The expansion of the architectural profession in the Potteries, as elsewhere, came at a time when increasing attention was being paid to industrial buildings. In 1834 there were two individuals listed as architects in the towns, both of whom were in Burslem. By 1879 there were twenty-four: eleven in Hanley and Shelton, five in Burslem, four in Longton, three in Stoke and one in Fenton.[7] Initially, their role in the design of factory architecture was still mainly confined to the potworks' façade, but as factory legislation forced a fresh look at the whole works, so the importance of design became greater and more challenging. The major architects of each of the towns, such as Robert Scrivener in Shelton, George Ford in Burslem and Charles Lynam in Stoke, became associated with the new factories in a way that had never been the case earlier.

There are two immediately striking points about the factories built in the last two decades of

the century. The first is the way in which the balance in priorities shifted from the presentational to the functional. At last it was properly recognised that efficiency and economy were relevant as much to the factory buildings themselves as to production. An Italianate style continued to be employed, less heavy than during the middle years of the century and closer to the earlier, more simple design. Now, however, the standing of the factory was regarded much more in terms of its efficient layout than the beauty of its façade. The Colonial Works in Fenton were seen as presenting 'an imposing as well as pleasing appearance', but though 'they are not without architectural pretensions...naturally utility and convenience are the chief desiderata in such a building'.[8] The striking orange-brick façade that the eminent Hanley architect Robert Scrivener gave to Twyford's sanitary works at Cliffe Vale was strongly Italianate in design, with boldly stated stonework detailing and a central fortress-style entrance. The effect was softened by the two

Plate 72
Entrance to Twyford's factory

Plate 73
Self-portrait, taken in about 1950, showing Mr W T Vickers, a sanitary ware worker at a Longport pottery, fettling a wash-basin

turrets and intricate detail of the central bay, and by the suggestion of the traditional pediment with ornamental proto-art nouveau lettering. The qualities of this frontage were notable, but subordinated to 'the compact and convenient arrangement of the various departments, their structural suitability to the purposes in hand, and the up-to-date perfection of the equipment', which provided for 'an even greater output than might be inferred from the imposing appearance of the exterior'.[9]

Despite technical advances made over the century, and the increase in output and scale of operations, there was no radical change in pottery factory design. Instead, the old arrangement was harnessed to new demands and requirements. In new factories, the old problems and defects could be ironed out, new facilities added and the whole updated, within the basic courtyard design.

Production still centred on the bottle oven, and while it did so, there would be no major architectural change.

It may be said that in general the largest of the later factories were larger than their early nineteenth-century counterparts, not so much in plan, though this also was the case, but by the greater use of three-storeyed structures. The rooms were supported by iron beams, some with iron columns for additional support, while the top floors still had wooden frameworks. The rooms tended to be larger than of old, with bigger windows and wider doors, which created a sense of space and light still visible in the extant factories of that date, such as the Alexandra Pottery in Tunstall (1886) and Eastwood Works in Hanley (*c*1887). The regulations of the 1891 and 1895 Factory and Working Acts included sufficient and well-distributed internal stone staircases. The use of disconnected buildings was advised, with bridging between, as was the practice of splitting factory buildings by a road and having a detached packing house (because of the high-risk straw inside). The division of large rooms into smaller compartments was not encouraged, though it was recognised that this might still be desirable for separating the distinct processes. The matter of trade secrets was still a consideration, as was the need to separate male and female workers.[10]

New branches of the industry, sanitary ware (Plate 73) and electrical insulators, were equipped with larger, open rooms by virtue of their product size. In the industry as a whole, there was also an increase in the size of workshops. The presence of machinery was not in itself responsible for this, since the equipment which the new machinery replaced occupied no less space. The eighteenth-century throwing wheel, operated by a rope pulley and wheel turned by a child or woman, was in its entirety larger than later models, whose design became increasingly compact during the nineteenth century. The jigger and jolley machines, which were used more frequently after the 1860s, were similarly small. In themselves, steam-powered mechanisms required no more space than was taken up by a child turning a handle, and the source of steam required only an additional room on site, for the boiler and engine.[11]

The importance of machinery to factory design was the rationalisation brought by semi-automation, and more particularly by steam power. Where it was possible to introduce machinery in the older factories, the disordered arrangement of buildings and conditions dictated the environment. The new ones, however, were organised around steam-powered machinery, and the example of order and efficiency thereby created set the standard for the whole industry.

IMPROVEMENTS IN WORKING CONDITIONS

Although the rooms were larger, it is difficult to generalise about the amount of space per worker by this stage compared to earlier in the century, partly because of the lack of sufficient information, and partly also because the space varied from factory to factory, and within each factory.[12] Moreover, contemporary descriptions can be misleading, in representing only the expectations of the time; potworks described as spacious and lofty by the Children's Employment Commission in 1841 might be deemed totally inadequate by the standards of the 1890s. The temptation to squeeze extra workers into a room was (in theory at least) curbed by factory legislation, and certainly the law appears to have been adhered to in the new, more spacious factories. At the new Burgess and Leigh factory at Middleport, those in the paint-ing room had around 700 cubic feet (19.8 cubic m) each; and at Twyford's it was asserted that twenty workers, in one of the workshops at least, had 1,700 cubic feet (48.2 cubic m) each, when formerly 'at least four men would have occuped such a space'.[13] The type of ware being produced inevitably influenced the amount of space allowed; far more was required in the sanitary ware factories than in the cup-making department of an ordinary factory. Nevertheless, given the definition in 1891 of overcrowding in a factory as less than 250 cubic feet (7.1 cubic m) per person, in provision if not always in reality the pottery industry emerged quite favourably.

Aside from this general aspect of health and safety, more attention was being paid to sanitary conditions in the factories. Many of the old potteries were found unfit for occupation and recommended for condemnation 'on the same principle as dwellings are declared uninhabit-able'.[14] Further experimentation with the heating systems had to take place because although the adoption of steam piping created enough warmth in the workshops, it had not been accompanied by measures for ventilation, resulting in overheating and rooms full of stagnant air. The provision of dining-rooms became compulsory, as did that of washing areas, both of which would need consideration in the design of future factories.

While government legislation was instrumental in bringing about these changes, philanthropy too continued to play an important part in raising standards and conditions in the factories, and in determining the enlightenment of their design. There was a wide diversity in the standing of manufacturers and in their relationship with their workers, which was visible in the similarly wide range of factories operating at this time. At one extreme was the self-made man who could not afford any structural outlay or his own premises, and who worked alongside his employees in dismal rented surroundings. This not uncommon situation is portrayed in Arnold Bennett's *Anna of the Five Towns*, where William Price and his father worked in the rented potworks described at the beginning of this chapter. Its frontage was 'irregular and huddled', and the Prices' office consisted of:

> a long narrow room, the dirtiest that Anna had ever seen. If such was the condition of the master's quarters, she thought, what must the workshops be like? The ceiling, which bulged downwards, was as black as the floor, which sank away from the middle till it was hollow like a saucer. The revolution of an engine somewhere below shook everything with a muffled thud. A greyish light came through one small window...[15]

Alongside these were the middling manufacturers who were renting works, such as Henry Mynors in the same novel. Mynors employed around one hundred people, but he was his own manager, and was proud of the efficiency of his works which went hand in hand with superiority in premises and in working conditions. His factory was:

> acknowledged to be one of the best, of its size, in the district – a model three oven bank. The architect of the 'Providence Works'...knew his business and the business of the potter, and he had designed the works with a view to the strictest economy of labour...The steam installation was complete: steam once generated had no respite; after it had exhausted itself in vitalizing fifty machines, it was killed by inches in order to dry the unfired ware and warm the dinners of the workpeople.[16]

At the upper end of the scale were the large manufacturers, whose money and close ties with the local area and its people led them to provide superior working environments. There was an ambivalent relationship between these manu-facturers and their employees. On the one hand there was a constant battle by the latter to improve wages and conditions of labour, and to eradicate injustices. On the other there was a strong sense of paternalism, which came through in factory planning as much as it did in social events, and in the provision of housing and public buildings. The concern was often genuine, but it was equally important that the good work should be seen to be done: the provision of improved factories was just one element of the philanthropic activities that were an indication of social standing in the community. In building the new works, the manufacturers were showing an interest in their workforce which had formerly only been shown for the ware.

Many of the manufacturers had had direct experience of working in factories, and though their own expression of concern was sometimes cushioned in self-esteem, the evidence for it comes through in the buildings themselves. Thomas Twyford recounted that as well as aiming at the greatest efficiency and economy in planning his works at Cliffe Vale, he had wanted

to remedy the insanitary conditions of all pottery works I had ever known, and so arrange the workshops for my men that the new works should be as healthy or even more healthy than their own homes. All the floors I had made of concrete, to prevent the heat from the lower stoves rising to the floors above; all divisional walls between the workshop and stove were built of brick, to prevent the heat from the stove getting to the men while at work, whereby the part that the men work in is kept as cool and at as even a temperature as the most fastidious person could desire. Each man has a window to himself, that he can open to admit fresh air, the windows being so arranged that there is no draught; there is a ventilator communicating with the outside...The stoves are all heated by exhaust steam, and air is admitted to them by means of ventilation; ventilating shafts are fitted in each stove, to draw away the foul air and the moisture of the atmosphere, which is so injurious to the men. These healthy shops mean more to workmen than can be described...It was seeing men suffering from this complaint [potter's rot] that roused my sympathy, and made me resolve that, if ever I built a pottery, everything should be done to obviate and do away with the causes of that terrible affliction...The men look different; they have no longer that ghastly pallor look on their faces that used to mark the potter...

In the dipping house was a 'wide, lofty, well-lighted and ventilated room, fitted with necessary water supply, soap, nail brushes, towels etc.' and the dippers were obliged to wear overalls and caps or hoods, which on leaving they hung 'in a room specially reserved for this purpose'.[17] Twyford was one of those manufacturers who not only followed regulations but pre-empted them, and who, by their knowledge of the workings, problems and abuses of factories, set the standards which future legislation would adopt.

The Middleport Pottery

The Middleport Pottery, still owned and run by the original family firm, is another factory typical of the later period and illustrative of many of the points made above. The partners Burgess and Leigh had started business in the 1850s in Tunstall, moved to the Central Pottery in Burslem in 1862, to the Hill Pottery in 1867, and finally in 1888 expanded yet again with their own new factory in Middleport.[18] They built it on the site of an old saggar manufactory by the Trent and Mersey Canal, in an undeveloped area which soon after the erection of the new factory gained a wharf and boatyard, and quickly became surrounded by terraced housing.

Described as 'the model pottery of Staffordshire', in architectural style and arrangement it was built in accordance with the work ethic of Victorian society.[19] It had none of the flamboyance in outward presentation of the earlier manufactories, but was designed purely for the greatest refinement and efficiency in production. At the same time, however, neither its design nor its structure was greatly removed from those of its forerunners.

The maxims of discipline, time and economy came through in the layout of the premises. Each department was quite separate and had its own independent access; as before, the upper floors in the 'making' range were supplied with external wooden staircases. Distance between the buildings

Plate 74
The Middleport Pottery, 1888

was kept to a minimum, wide enough for a cart to pass through and for the easy flow of workers and ware, but not enough to demand time-consuming running about.

The two-storeyed front range of the Middleport factory along Port Street is impressive in its length, but not ostentatious (Plate 74). Like the rest of the factory, it was built of plain red brick with a tiled roof. Its length is relieved by

five evenly spaced gabled bays, four of them with lunette windows. The other, forming the arched coach entrance to the works at the northern end, was the focal point in decorative treatment, with patterned relief tiles defining the pediment and relief brick panels forming the background to an ornamental emblem, date and the name 'Middleport Pottery' (Plate 75). Inside this building, the entrance hall has a floor of patterned tiles, the

Plate 75
The Middleport Pottery, looking through the main entrance to the workshops and canal beyond

staircase ornamental wrought-iron banisters. The offices occupying this end of the range were comfortable in fittings and features, such as the doors and windows with patterned coloured glass insets; but the overall impression is one of business rather than show.

The old quadrangular plan was used to form the basis for a quite innovative arrangement. Firms

Figure 5
*Burgess and Leigh,
Middleport*

5a *ground-floor plan*

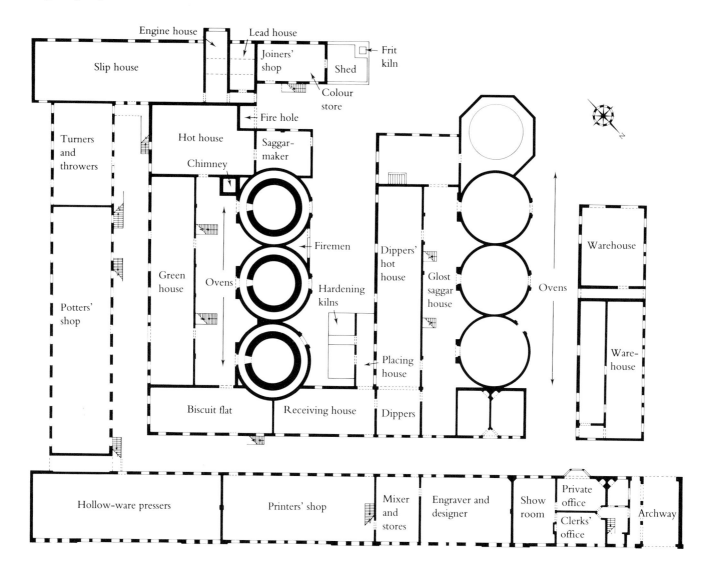

5b *front elevation*

which had expanded on their original sites had a confusion of wasteful movement based around the ovens. In starting afresh for an already expanded business, Burgess and Leigh were able to incorporate the ovens into the line of production rather than allowing them to dictate it. The difficulty of achieving an efficient forward flow of a wide range of ware was solved by having a series of parallel ranges within the quadrangular plan. Although there were still quite separate buildings for the different stages, they were in strict order of sequence and there was only a small distance between them across the yard. The plan catered for sideways movement, with bridging between the range across the end of these buildings and the front range (Figure 5).

Raw materials were unloaded from the canal at the rear corner of the site and could be kept there, outside, until needed. The row of buildings here consisted of frit kiln, small colour store, lead house, joiners' shop, engine house (built around the steam engine, which supplied power for the whole factory) and three-storeyed slip house, which had heavy slip-making machinery, on the ground floor, glaze mill, mould-makers' room and first hollow-ware pressing shop above, and a narrow staircase leading up to a block and case store on the second floor.

At right angles to these buildings was a two-storeyed 'making' range, with rooms supported by iron columns and a wooden framework. On the ground floor were throwing and turning, and jigger and jolley rooms, while above were two more pressing shops. A basement below is thought to have been used as a mould store (Plate 76) but was possibly for clay. The 'making' processes spread from this area into the end of the front range, as well as to the end of the rear building as has already been described.

From here, the pots passed across the cobbled yard (Plate 77) to a parallel two-storeyed biscuit range, which contained the green house, saggar house, placing area, hot house, biscuit warehouse and the biscuit overlooker's office. The office had an oriel window from which movement between the ranges could be supervised. The biscuit ovens were built in a row along the side of the building, with direct access into it.

Next came the glost range where decorating took place, extending into the centre of the front range for printing. The designers and engravers were also accommodated in this area of the front range. An open, shelved lift for ware operated between the two floors of the glost building. In compliance with new legislation, Burgess and Leigh included a communal washing and bath-house in a basement at one end of the decorating

Plate 76
The Middleport Pottery: mould store

Plate 77
The Middleport Pottery: the cobbled alleyway between ranges of workshops

Plate 78
*The Middleport Pottery:
the washroom and bath*

quarry-tiled floors. At the other end of the range was a mess room, with separate eating areas for male and female workers, each with its own fireplace. There was no direct access from the dipping rooms, which lessened the temptation to go straight in without washing.

The following range was composed of warehouses, also spreading to the front range at first-floor level. Given the wide variety of ware being produced, for markets both at home and abroad, considerable space was required for this final stage. In the warehouses the pots could be sorted on the wooden floors, spread out for stock checking and the gathering of orders. They also served as display rooms

> *exhibiting an endless array of the varied patterns in tea, dinner, toilet and pheasant or common sets, some brown, some white, some glittering with gold and brilliant enamels, and printed in blues, greens, pinks, or the natural colours of flowers, foliage etc…*
>
> *In a word, those desirous of seeing a truly* fin de siècle *museum of the finest things in modern pottery could not do better than ask this courteous firm for permission to have a look at its warehouses.*[20]

block (Plate 78). Eight relief-moulded wash-basins stood underneath windows at ground level, with a bath in a small adjoining room. These rooms were tiled throughout with white glazed tiles and had

The showroom proper was in London, by now common practice for Potteries firms. (In 1883

Figure 6
*35 South Wolfe Street,
Stoke-on-Trent*

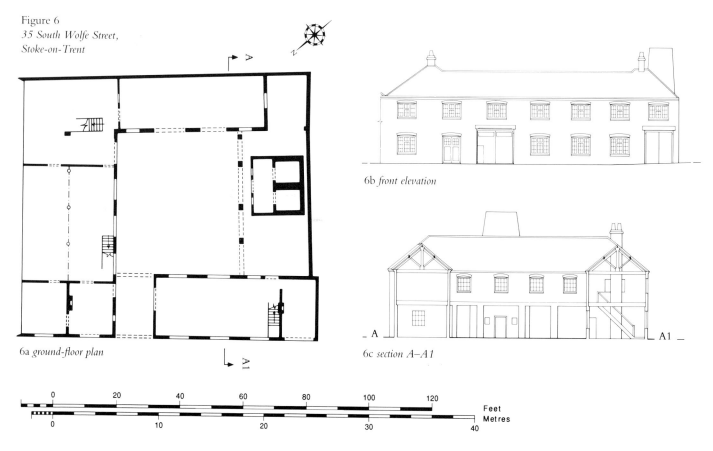

6a *ground-floor plan*

6b *front elevation*

6c *section A–A1*

sixty-eight firms had show and sample rooms in the capital. Only seven ran their own; the rest were operated by agents who acted either for one or for several firms.)[21] The packing house was separated from the warehouses by a road running down from the front entrance to the canal, and finished ware could be taken straight on to barges, or out by road.

There were small courtyard potteries, such as the Victoria Works in Stoke, being built even at this date which add nothing to the history of architectural development but serve to show the variety in scale and facilities which still existed in the industry. Some of them were decorating works, such as that built at South Wolfe Street in Stoke around 1890 (Figure 6)[22] and the Smithfield Pottery, built in Lower Mollart Street, Hanley, in 1880 (Plate 79). The plan of the Smithfield Works was tempered to fit into the site (Figure 7). The plot of land was a small, neglected one on the outskirts of Hanley's urban development, on which Thomas Hinde, a rope manufacturer, built two rows of terraced houses. The potworks, a part of his plan, was built to slot in between two sets of housing, and he let it to the potter Charles Barlow as a decorating works at an annual rent of £27, together with a house next to the site.[23] Like the

pottery in South Wolfe Street, it could easily be mistaken for one of much earlier origin, built around a part-cobbled courtyard and with a single bottle oven rising out from one corner.

Plate 79
The Smithfield Pottery, Hanley, 1880

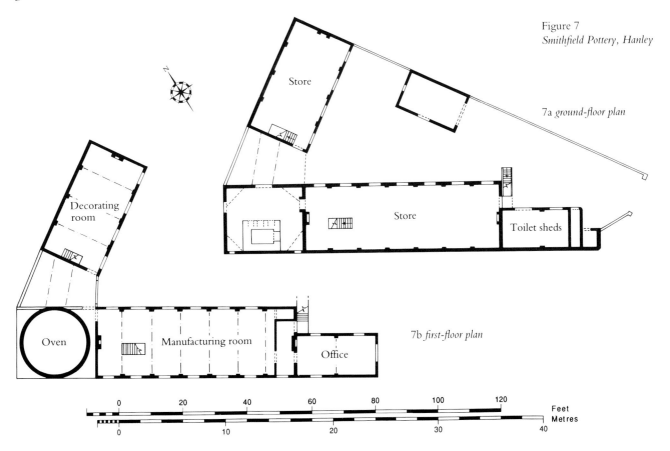

Figure 7
Smithfield Pottery, Hanley

7a *ground-floor plan*

7b *first-floor plan*

The layout of the Smithfield Pottery was simple, mainly consisting of long, open workrooms on each floor. In addition to this, the longer west range had a narrower end nearest the site entrance, which comprised an office on the first floor and store below. Two lean-to brick toilet sheds adjoined the end of the building. The office, with windows to three sides, and overlooking entrance and works, was entered by an external staircase. A wooden partition formed a small area between this and the manufacturing room, so that each had its independent access from the stairs. The works are so small that aside from this, room allocation and arrangement are not significant.

Plate 80
Victoria Place, Fenton

The main ground floor in the western range was designed with fitted racks along its length, and was the store for incoming biscuit-fired ware. Decorating materials were kept in the ground-floor room in the other main building, and prepared for use in the room above. They could then be taken straight through into the decorating room to be used. Internally and externally, the buildings displayed the characteristics of the basic earlier potworks: unplastered walls and exposed framework. The rooms were quite dark, the more so since most of the workshop areas had windows on only one side – though the important decorating room was well lit. Heating came from plain, open fireplaces in each room.

In such a mixed fashion the pottery industry entered the twentieth century. Some of the small potteries of the late nineteenth century are still extant, while the large ones too are numerous and continue to function as working factories, their size and nature allowing quite easy adaptation to modern methods. Their construction on strategic sites has left them clearly visible and a part of the heritage of each of the six towns.

MANUFACTURERS' HOUSES

By the end of the century there was an even greater range in the status of manufacturers than earlier. Those at the top end of the scale moved out not only from the town centres but, because of the gradual infill of surrounding space in the second half of the century, right into the countryside. Michael Daintry Hollins moved from Fenton Hall to Springfield Hall, Chorlton, and finally to Whitmore Hall, where he died in 1898. Thomas Twyford lived successively at Shelton, Endon, Moor House in Biddulph, and then followed Hollins at Whitmore Hall. Colin Minton Campbell, who had lived with his father-in-law Herbert Minton at Longfield Cottage in Hartshill, then moved out to Woodseat, near Uttoxeter. John Aynsley left Longton to live at Portland House, Blythe Bridge, while his former partner and prominent potter, Sampson Bridgwood, lived just outside the Potteries, at Lightwood.[24] This time, when the manufacturers moved to country seats, it was not to erect their own houses but to take up residence in existing ones, built not for their predecessors in the industry but for country gentry and landowners amidst their rural estates.

These men were in the minority. Most manufacturers remained in the district, in the towns themselves or, more usually, in the developing suburbs. An additional opportunity for such development came with the laying out of the public parks – Longton in 1888, Hanley between 1892 and 1897, Burslem in 1894, and Tunstall between 1897 and 1908.[25] Building immediately began on the surrounding roads, those houses fronting the parks being occupied by the middle range of manufacturers, pottery managers, modellers and artists, and various other trades and professions.

WORKERS' HOUSING

While improvements had been made in workers' housing, the new houses were as yet a minority amongst the mass of older ones which had deteriorated since the reports of the 1850s. In 1872, Longton was condemned by a Board of Health doctor as 'the closest, worst ventilated, worst drained, and generally as respects its surface, its dwellings, and its atmosphere, the dirtiest and most polluted', but each of the other towns had their black spots.[26] The problems of ineffective sanitation and structural design faults were compounded by insufficiency: the still-expanding population had outpaced the supply of cheap houses for the poorer workers, so that crowding had become a feature in all the towns.

Nevertheless, the guidelines of central government, increased public awareness and the activity of the local boards of health resulted in a slow but steady rise in standards. The consequence of by-laws was uniformity in design and on the whole the complete lack of imagination displayed by speculative builders. The latter were responsible for much of the building during this period, with a few notable groups provided by the pottery manufacturers. One interesting example of the latter is the development at Victoria Place in Fenton, erected by the manufacturer William Meath Baker in 1887 (Plates 80 and 81).

Victoria Place, Fenton

The Baker family had occupied the manufactory along the present City Road since at least the beginning of the nineteenth century, and were probably responsible for a row of early cottages adjoining it on the lower side. The later triangular development, further toward Longton, stood in complete contrast to these dwellings, reflecting the enormous wealth and status which the family had achieved in the locality. Around fifty houses were built together, replacing all except two cottages of a development which had consisted partly of a courtyard grouping. The old cottages were small humble brick and tile dwellings; the new buildings were elaborate High Victorian ones, in orange-red brick with façades rich in relief decoration.

The superiority ended inside, where the houses were fairly typical of the later nineteenth century. Each house had the standard front parlour, 12 feet by 11 feet (3.6 m by 3.3 m), kitchen, 12 feet (3.6 m) square, and a back kitchen, 10 feet 6 inches by 7 feet (3.2 m by 2.1 m). On the ground floor, the staircase divided the front and rear rooms, and led up to three bedrooms, two with fireplaces. The rooms were high, with ceilings at 9 and 9 feet 6 inches (2.7 m and 2.9 m), and door heights of 6 feet 6 inches (2 m). The only signs of decoration in the house surveyed were the blue and red quarry tiles on the floor in the kitchen and the cornicing in the parlour. At the rear of the house, in a yard paved with blue brick, was a lean-to coal-shed and, at the bottom of the yard, a water-closet.

The activity of the Baker family in Fenton is typical of developments throughout the Potteries, in general terms if not in precise detail. Bourne, Baker and Bourne had established themselves as manufacturers in Fenton by the early nineteenth century, and had expanded until they owned a very large potworks site adjoined by a modest

number of workers' cottages. They had accumulated land to the extent of owning much of Fenton, and had built two large manufacturers' houses overlooking their works. By the later years of the century, the descendants of the original manufacturers had moved from the district but their money and interests still lay there. The Victoria Place housing development reflected their status and presence as much as ever, but the community was left more than this as a reminder of the family. In acknowledgement of the wealth which the Bakers had gained in Fenton, William Meath Baker provided a new town hall, in 1888, and rebuilt Christ Church, in 1890, forming the core of the town centre to which he made further contributions in the early years of the present century.[27] Throughout the Potteries are such memorials to the success of the pottery industry and the fortunes of its leaders.

Plate 81
*Numbers 10 and 12
Victoria Place, Fenton*

Chapter 6

THE EARLY TWENTIETH CENTURY: FUNCTIONALISM AND BEYOND

Only the still geometry
Of the quiet canal
The calm symmetry of the empty kilns
These great mute wounds
The desires stilled
Stand waiting to be broken open

Arthur Berry, *Landscape*

By the beginning of the twentieth century, the population of 234,000 was accommodated in an area of just over 11,000 acres (4,450 ha), which it shared with potworks, brick and tile works, coal mines and quarries; not to mention the large areas made useless by their liability to subsidence.

THE 'GARDEN CITY' MOVEMENT IN THE POTTERIES

Several schemes for middle-class housing were carried out, continuing the extension of suburban areas. The most significant architecturally was the Penkhull Garden Village, begun in 1910. In conception, the scheme directly followed the principles of the national movement, which had been established in reaction against the crowded, polluted industrial towns, in favour of the rural idyll with its associated lifestyle and values (Plate 82). With the backing of local dignitaries such as

Earl Harrowby and the Mayor of Stoke, the group also gained the considerable help and co-operation of the national Co-Partnership Tenants Ltd, benefiting from the skills and experience of its prominent members. Barry Parker, a key protagonist of the new movement and joint architect with Raymond Unwin of Letchworth Garden City, oversaw the preliminary work at Penkhull, though a local firm of architects, W Campbell and Sons of Hanley, designed the houses. The Birmingham builder Frank Williams, who had established his reputation in Birmingham 'garden' projects, was brought in as site manager from 1914 to 1929. The Penkhull Society was also able to buy tools and building materials cheaply through its involvement with the Co-Partnership Tenants Ltd.[1]

The site chosen was one of thirty-eight freehold acres on an elevated rural spot between Stoke and Newcastle, carefully selected so that the prevailing wind would blow smoke from the pottery factories away from the estate. The emphasis was on the communal, in arrangement and facilities. 'Instead of the buildings being mere endless rows, or the repetition of isolated houses having no connection one with the other, they will naturally gather themselves into groups and the groups again clustered round the greens will form large units.' There would be ten or twelve houses per acre, ninety-five houses in all, varying in size and design, all with large gardens, so that 'the people will develop a sense of home life and interest in nature and obtain security against the evil arising through living in unhealthy and crowded areas'.[2]

The houses were rustic in style, with steeply pitched roofs and gables, small-paned casement windows, dormer windows, steps to the front doors and protruding wooden sills and lintels. They were designed so that maximum use was made of natural light by the provision of bays, and glass insets in the doors. In contrast to the long, narrow terraced houses with their string of

Plate 82
Penkhull Garden Village, 1910

Plate 83
*Aerial view of Longton
(photograph taken between
1927 and 1932)*

outbuildings at the rear, the Penkhull houses had a compact, box-like plan. Also, the emphasis had shifted to the rear of the house and the secluded garden area there. The extra width of the house allowed a 'wash-up' room, larder and fuel store. There was an upstairs bathroom, hall and landing, and a fireplace in each room.

Little was being done to house the ordinary working people during this time. No industrial villages were established by employers, and the only council even to consider a model workers' dwelling scheme was Hanley; this, however, was never carried out. It was not until after World War I that a new phase of activity began in the Potteries, with the Borough Council taking advantage of the government's huge subsidy to provide 'homes fit for heroes'.

Investigation of possible sites proved that it would be a difficult task, since the whole area was scattered with schraff (pottery waste) heaps and pit mounds, and the land was liable to subsidence. In any case, the idea was to move people out of the unhealthy town centres. The only solution was to look beyond to land outside the borough, 'some of the best land in the county', and to extend the boundaries, which in fact happened in 1922.[3] Council housing estates involving several hundreds of houses were built at Meir and Trent Vale, and, under the Wheatley Act of 1921, at Abbey Hulton, Milton and Basford.[4]

As happened elsewhere, the local authority adopted the principles of the garden village and city movement in its housing developments, in this case directly looking to the Penkhull Garden Village. The new council estates were similarly set in rural environments, had the same low density and grouping of houses, were set around central greens, and had the combination of semi-detached and terraced dwellings. The houses were set back from the road and had large gardens. Local architects were employed by the Council to undertake their design, building work was put out to tender to local firms, and local materials were used in the construction. Care was taken to use these to the best effect: 'the pleasant general appearance [of the estate] will be accentuated by varying the bricks and tiles in the separate blocks, so as to avoid as far as possible any monotony that might arise'.[5] The houses shared the rustic style of the Penkhull estate, but with more uniformity and economy shown in their design and construction.[6] Even with such economies, however, the rents of 9s 6d to 15s were far too high for working people to be able to afford. As one ex-serviceman wrote: 'It will be much more simple to make the houses fit for heroes than to make heroes to live in them. Few heroes are millionaires.'[7] Only the more fortunate working families were able to enjoy the comfort and pleasure of the new estates, while the poorest remained in the terraced streets of the borough.

'FUNCTIONALISM' IN THE POTWORKS

While slum clearance took place and new housing replaced the worst areas in the Potteries, the number and size of factories altered very little (Plate 83). There were around 500 works, with those of medium size employing 100 to 400 workers. Units were kept relatively small, with the

99

large firms, such as Johnsons, Adams and Woods, broken up rather than operating on single massive sites for which there was no need.[8]

Architectural interest in efficiency and economy had developed naturally into twentieth-century functionalism. Ironically, while in scale and sophistication of production they were far removed from pre-industrial potworks, in their outward plainness and lack of show the new factories shared more with their predecessors than at any stage in the intervening years. There was little activity in factory building, with firms tending to take over existing works rather than building afresh. Where additions were made, they offered no radical change, and improvement was in refinement rather than fundamental design. It was reported of new workshops, such as those built at the Florence Works in Longton, 1914, for example, that they were 'of sound construction, with the most approved type of impermeable flooring, in every way complying with the stringent Home Office regulations', and that their main qualities were their 'spaciousness and airiness'.[9] Externally, the buildings were anonymous, less inspired and individualistic than their forerunners, and of no architectural note. The warehouse range that was added to the Falcon Works in Sturgess Street, Stoke, between 1902 and 1905 is such a structure, a plain brick building of three storeys.[10] Its one concession to decoration is a relief plaque of a falcon on the end

wall facing the road. Internally, the large open rooms are supported on the ground and first floors by a combination of brick pillars and iron columns supporting iron girders. The second floor is open to the roof, with a traditional wooden framework.

With the exception of the lettering on the Cliffe Vale works (see p 88), there is no sign of the Potteries having taken up the art nouveau style, though one or two of the associated manufactories did so. Appropriately for its business in supplying decorating transfers to the industry, one of these was Ratauds, built in Hanley in 1914 and demolished to make way for the town's by-pass in 1986 (Plate 84). Another was the colour manufactory of Keeling and Walker, built around 1907 near to the Colonial Works in Fenton. Still run by the original family, it has retained not only its striking façade but also an immaculate interior, with decorative entrance, and glass-partitioned offices with panelled walls.

A RETURN TO 'HAND-CRAFT' IN THE POTTERIES

Welfare work in the factories became an issue with growing awareness of the dehumanising effect of the Industrial Revolution and appreciation of the old working environment. 'As industrial concerns had grown larger and larger', it was reported in the *Pottery Gazette* in 1914, 'so the human element had been gradually crushed out.

Plate 84
*Ratauds Ceramic
Transfers, Hanley, 1914
(demolished in 1986)*

Plate 85
Moorcroft Pottery factory,
Cobridge, 1913–20

On our modern conditions it would be an advantage if some of the older conditions could be re-introduced'.[11] The nostalgia was for human relationships rather than physical conditions. The ideal would be to restore the human relationships and happiness in work associated with the old potworks, while at the same time providing all the improved facilities for eating, sanitation, lighting, heating and clothing which had been achieved gradually in more recent years.

Moorcroft Pottery

The ultimate in modernity, both architecturally and socially, made its appearance in a quite untypical factory, that of Moorcroft in Cobridge. Studio rather than factory, it not only reverted to the purely functional style of pre-industrial potteries, but was geared to completely hand-crafted pottery-making and a small number of employees. William Moorcroft had been employed as a designer at the Washington Works in Burslem, a conglomeration of nineteenth-century buildings with all the inherent inconveniences and poor working conditions that they represented. When the new Art Pottery department there closed in 1913, he decided to continue on his own, taking around twenty decorators and craftsmen and forming his own company. With his wife Florence, one of the country's first female factory

inspectors, he built a small factory, which was completed for production in ten weeks (Plate 85).[12] The present, extended larger form of the factory appears to be as it was originally conceived, but with building work disrupted by World War I, it was eventually achieved in three stages: the core, including one bottle oven in 1913, and two surrounding structures, together with two more ovens, in 1915 and 1919–20.

The site chosen by Moorcroft was alongside the North Staffordshire railway and overlooked Cobridge Park, a position selected as being on the highest open space available. The factory itself occupied only a quarter of the site, which was 'surrounded by trees and shrubs to form a pleasant boundary'.[13] A local architect, A A Longden, designed it from proposals drawn up by Moorcroft himself, the combined product of Florence Moorcroft's influence and ideas as factory inspector and William's own experience. The resulting building reflected Moorcroft's adherence to the humane ideals and philosophy of the Arts and Craft Movement and the most up-to-date standards in factory design.

It comprised a single one-storeyed building that was quite featureless externally, presenting a plain, windowless wall to the outside world. The main entrance, at the side, was equally unpretentious; only the ornamental wrought-iron

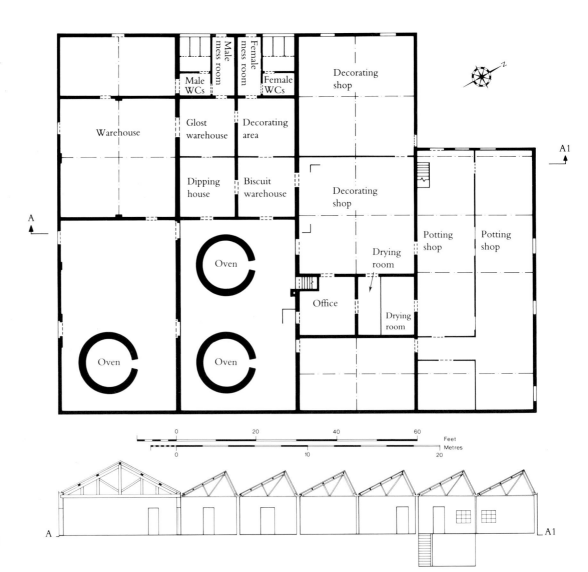

Figure 8
*Moorcroft Pottery,
Cobridge*

8a *ground-floor plan*

8b *cross-section A–A1*

entrance gates gave the premises any external decoration, together with a bold name sign announcing the firm's presence.

Moorcroft was one of the first in the Potteries to build a single-storey works (Figure 8). The factory's layout included the division of other small potworks: potting shops, decorating rooms, drying rooms, mould store, dipping and warehouse rooms, and three bottle ovens within the building. As with other small concerns, the existence of clay suppliers meant that there was no need for self-sufficiency in the way of clay preparation. While others were introducing more and more machinery into their cramped nineteenth-century buildings, however, Moorcroft's craft (as opposed to industrial) orientation meant that there were few concessions to machine power in the building. Rather than steam, a heating vault underneath the office supplied a coke-fired heating system, the coke being tipped through a chute outside the office straight into the

vault. A system of pipes ran through the building with radiators in the shops, supplemented by cast-iron stove pots.

The factory was built in the same years as the new Health and Safety Act and fully complied with its requirements. The single-storey arrangement meant that the hazardous practice of carrying materials and ware up and down from one floor to another, which William Moorcroft had witnessed at the Washington Works, was no longer necessary; it also ruled out the problem of dust filtering through from the upper rooms. Government specifications of 1913 demanded that floors either be impervious or else wooden 'with a thoroughly smooth and sound surface, constructed in such a substantial manner as to be free from permanent sag, and maintained in such repair that they can be properly cleaned by a moist method'.[14] The workshops at Moorcroft's factory were provided with slanting concrete floors which could be swilled down: each had gutters and drainage grids. There were toilets and mess rooms for each sex, set aside from the workshops, a facility which, although required by law, was still by no means common.

The lighting also was innovative. Initially, the only windows on the sides of the building were those in the staff toilets and mess rooms. All other light came from skylights or 'northern lights' (Plate 86), fitted diagonally in a series of parallel projections along the length of the building, to give the workers maximum light. Skylighting employed in later nineteenth-century factories simply involved an insertion into the traditional roof. In Moorcroft's works, however, it helped shape, and visually affected, the total design. Ventilation came from these windows, some of which were made to open, and from slatted vents in the roof.

The factory was designed to satisfy the requirements of both efficiency and good working conditions. There was no showroom, and the office was modest in size and in fittings. There was no element of surveillance, probably because of the factory's small scale and because Mr Moorcroft himself took an active and central role in the production. Such involvement also meant that, unlike some factory owners, he was fully aware of, and sympathetic to, working conditions and the suitability of his premises.

The street front of the building had a small wooden porch at the side of the office, while workers entered through a door at the side of the factory. Clay was delivered at the back, where there was an entrance to the potting shop and stairs leading straight down to a clay cellar; glaze material came in directly to the dipping room. Throughout the building, doors were significantly wider than those in earlier factories, making passage and carriage much easier. All materials arrived by horse and cart, and finished ware was transported similarly to Hanley station. Coals for the bottle oven came from the Sneyd Colliery nearby.

Other factories, of larger scale and built for traditional production, were less informal and less progressive. Their outward uniformity and lack of charm left them with none of the character of those belonging to the previous century, and when the tunnel kiln replaced the bottle oven the uniqueness of the potworks was lost for ever. In 1938 the firm of Josiah Wedgwood and Sons began the construction of a new purpose-built factory and community complex outside the village of Barlaston, several miles from the Potteries.[15] However, this was an example which was not followed until recent years, with the establishment of such firms as Twyford's (now Caradon Twyford Ltd) at Alsager and Staffordshire Potteries (now Staffordshire Tableware Ltd) at Meir. The pottery industry has remained largely within the city.

New building continues to take place on old potwork sites, and the industry operates within a range of buildings just as it has always done. The surviving cramped, ill-lit nineteenth-century workshops provide a strong contrast with the spacious open areas of the twentieth-century shop floors, although the latter have lost the intimacy of their predecessors. The range of technology used in the factories is equally striking, with individual

hand work to be seen alongside production-line manufacturing, and computerised, even laser-operated kilns. The old-established family firms have now almost without exception been swallowed by huge outside conglomerates, which in some cases have no past experience of the pottery industry. At the same time, however, the 1980s saw the revival of the small-scale pottery manufacturers, who took on the ramshackle premises of earlier firms as a starting-base for their enterprise. Together, the mixture of crumbling and new buildings, craft and high-technology pottery-making, and financial giants and small employers, represent the current state of the industry, and combine to ensure the continued hum and bustle of the Potteries into the future.

Plate 86
Moorcroft Pottery: painting shop with skylights

Appendix

THE POT OVEN

There were no tall chimneys, no factory buildings frowning above the streets; but only a fantastic collection of narrow-necked jars or bottles peeping above the house-tops on every side, looking as if giant biblical characters, after a search for oil or wine, had popped them there, among the dwarf streets. These, of course, are the pottery kilns and ovens...Without these great bottles of heat, there would be no Potteries. They represent a very heart and soul of the district, as you very soon learn; and unless you are prepared to take a deep and lasting interest in what happens inside those ovens, it would be better for you to take the first train anywhere.

Priestley 1934, p 199

Plate 87
Kiln at the Moorcroft Pottery, Cobridge

The pot ovens have been mentioned briefly but merit a separate explanation in their own right. The familiar bottle-shaped pot oven developed from the domed multi-flued up-draught kiln of the thirteenth century as found at Sneyd Green (see p 6), with heat being directed up amongst the pots through the flues.[1] By the seventeenth century, these temporary clay structures had been replaced by semi-permanent ones (see p 8), and we are told that in an oven of pots 'about eight feet high and six feet wide, of a round, copped form', a firing would take twenty-four hours, with a cooking period of ten hours.[2]

At some stage it became the practice to have one or more iron bands or 'bontings' around the oven to help keep the structure intact during continual expansion and contraction (Plate 87). There is a reference to a 'girdle' for an oven in Longton in 1709, and to 'oven bonds' among a Shelton potter's equipment in 1722.[3] Inside the oven, glazed pots were separated by kiln props, and by the end of the seventeenth century they were being placed in clay boxes or 'saggars' (Plates 88 and 89), to allow stacking without contact and to protect the ware from the flames.

The main development came in the form of the hovel, the structure encasing the oven, which helped to conserve heat loss and prevented damaging draughts through the oven, while at the same time assisting an overall upward draught through its chimney. It also provided protection for pots when they were brought to the oven, and for the fireman responsible for fuelling and tending the firing, though this was probably more an incidental advantage rather than a reason for the introduction of the hovel. Of two kilns discovered in Hanley dating from *c*1700, one had no hovel while the other showed traces of one. The first kiln had three brick courses and was bonded with red clay. It had six to seven fire-boxes, an unpaved floor and an external diameter of 12 feet (3.7 m). The other shared the same number of fireboxes, unpaved floor and clay bonding, and had a diameter of 10 feet (3.1 m).[4] Once the hovel had been adopted, the oven retained its dome, and the hovel itself took on the familiar bottle shape.

A court case from 1718–19 provides some useful information on the kilns, on the problems which they generated, and a hint as to the gradual raising in height of the chimney which took place in the eighteenth century. The case concerned a Shelton potter, John Middleton, who was blamed for causing his neighbour's building to burn down and annoying him with the smoke from his oven. John Middleton had a 'kiln or byler' within his workshop which was 'used in and about the boyling of clay and preparing it for making of pots', and which was thought responsible for the fire; he also had his pot oven, which stood outside the building, for firing the ware. He was ordered to take down the former and replace it with a large 'tunnell or pipe', of comparative size to that of his offended neighbour and fellow potter, Joshua Astbury. He was also made to raise the 'case' of his oven outside to the height of 9 yards (8.2 m) – a considerable height – so that the smoke emitting from it would no longer be a nuisance.[5]

Plate 88
A saggar-maker at work

Plate 89
The backyard of terraced houses in John Street, Longton, with a dividing wall built of oven saggars (photograph taken in the 1920s)

A more vivid account of the pollution from the ovens during the early eighteenth century comes from an author writing in the early nineteenth century. He stated that there had been around twenty ovens in the parish of Burslem with the custom of a uniform firing among

FIRING A POTTER'S OVEN.   S.8.

Plate 90
'Firing a potter's oven'
c1900, Longton

potters, starting on Thursday evening and reaching optimum temperature on Saturday morning, at which stage salt would be thrown into the oven to form a glaze on the pots (Plate 90).

> *This occasioned such immense and constant volumes of smoke, as literally to envelope the whole neighbourhood: and it was not unfrequent for passengers to mistake their way, and run against each other, during the continuance of this process. The scene which presented itself upon these occasions, has been not inaptly compared to the emissions of Etna or Vesuvius...*[6]

The erection of an oven was a skilled and crucial piece of craftsmanship. Until the later part of the eighteenth century it is not certain whether a bricklayer was brought in to build it or if the potter himself was involved. When a Barlaston clerk let a house and potworks in Lane Delph to potters Thomas Dakin and William Chatterley in 1709, an inventory of the workhouse contents included 'one set of Oven Brick, Materials for one kiln, one poker and drawing iron, and one Girdle for Oven', as if the landlord was supplying a type of self-assembly kit from which to construct their own kiln. There was already a kiln attached to the workhouse, however, and it seems likely that these materials were provided to repair or replace it when necessary.[7] The life of an oven was short,

and landlords usually specified in leases that they would not be responsible for its repair.

Attempts to improve the design of the kiln can be found as early as the seventeenth century. In 1635 a patent was taken out by a Captain Thornesse Francke, on an invention for

> *The Saveing Of Fewell, Labour, Ireon, And Tyme...in kylnes for makeing brickes, tyles, earthen potts, and lyme...effected and donne by altering the formes of the melting furnaces, and by contracting the ayre, and causing and bringing in wynd into the sayd furnacies, wch shall make the fyers burne with as much vyolence as any blast whatsoever...*

The patent is an intriguing one, for the improved kiln was also of a type able to be used by brewers, dyers, soap boilers, salt makers and metal and glass workers. It was purported to avoid 'The Annoyance Of Smoke', to operate 'without either water blaste or foote blaste', to require less ground than was currently used for ponds and water courses, and to save the transport costs of 'carrying the material to melting'.[8]

The pressure of a growing industry, and the more precise temperature control demanded by new clays, types of ware and decoration in the eighteenth century, must have meant that consideration continued to be given to the design of kilns, both in technical detail and in overall shape. Unfortunately, there is no documentary proof of experimentation other than by Josiah Wedgwood, whose scientific interests led him to the important invention in 1782 of a pyrometer to measure the heat inside the oven.[9] Samuel Smiles, nineteenth-century admirer of all enterprising individuals, included in his flattering account of Wedgwood that he had: 'pulled down one after another [of his ovens] in order to find the furnace that would bake his earthenware and melt his glazes. This cost him a great deal of money, but he conquered the difficulty by his usual perseverance'.[10]

However biased, the description raises the question of cost, which was an obvious deterrent to the majority of potters who could not afford the time, withdrawal of working kilns or direct expenses involved in such trials, even if they might benefit in the long run by improved economic efficiency. The size of kiln chosen is equally important. In terms of space, financial outlay and cost of firing, it was more desirable to have one or two very big kilns than several small ones, but the drawbacks to such a choice were that the kilns took longer to fill and each firing risked a larger number of wasted pots. Only potters with sufficiently large sites and available money were able to do as Wedgwood did, which was to build an extra, smaller kiln that required less pots, could be fired more quickly and used for whatever type of firing was required. In a letter dated 1769, Wedgwood wrote:

We find our large Ovens very inconvenient for Vases, I mean in point of time as it is near two months' work to fill the bisket oven. I am therefore building a small one of a new construction which is only to hold two or three basketfull, say £100 worth or so of Vases, it is to be a very good natur'd Oven and either bisket, Glost or Enamel as occasion serves.[11]

By its nature the pot oven's form invited challenge, both as a matter of pride and of aesthetics. Simeon Shaw maintained that in the mid eighteenth century, salt-glaze potter John Mitchell of Burslem had enlarged his premises, and 'as only One hovel was still thought requisite for all who made salt glaze ware, the strife among the potter who should excel in the size height of the hovel, caused him to erect the most enormorsly [sic] wide and high one ever attempted to be built'. He continued:

The largest hovel ever attempted, was finished at Burslem by John Shrigley, in 1765. Many persons witnessed the laying of the last brick, but no sooner was this completed, than the fabric began to crack and open, and in a few minutes the whole was level with the ground, and the builders escaped, most miraculously, by sudden descent. This caused low hovels to be adopted.[12]

The potential of the kiln shape caught the imagination of Wedgwood when planning his new works at Etruria: 'The Hovels may be... or...or...or...you see my line is at an end or I do not know where I should stop building hovels, and they may be decorated with Facias, blank windows etc. at very little expense.'[13] The bottle shape of the hovel, which eventually became standard, was a result of raising the height of the chimney to clear and draw the smoke.

Though builders were being employed by this date, the presence of only one man under the heading of 'oven builder' in Allbut's 1802 directory, in Burslem, suggests that the raising of ovens and hovels came within the field of the ordinary builder, who would have developed the required skills for this specialised construction. The placing of a kiln on the potworks site came from the logical decision as to its ease of access in relation to the workhouses, warehouses and fuel supplies, and the builder may also have considered the stress tolerance of the ground it was to stand on, and the direction of prevailing winds.

Uncertainties about the early kilns are to some extent resolved for the nineteenth century onwards, as not only are there complete surviving examples, but there is also the oral evidence of the oven builders and kiln workers who have first-hand knowledge of the structures and their operation.

According to an account of 1845, the bricks at that date were made from shale marl and slate clay, which would have been available locally, while the mortar was made from a mixture of either fireclay and sharp sand or china clay and borax. The whole was sealed together in the first firing.[14] Later on, Stourbridge bricks frequently became used for part of the kiln, while the rest was made up of common brick. Plan specifications for one of the Moorcroft kilns in 1915 state that the interior of the oven was to have mainly common firebricks, while Stourbridge firebricks were to be used ten courses high over the arches inside the fire bags. The fire bags themselves were to be built six courses with Stourbridge bricks and finished with common firebricks. The oven base was to be of common bricks covered with Stourbridge bricks.[15] According to a local oven builder, the mortar mixture used in the early twentieth century was three parts black ash, two

Plate 91
*Decorative treatment to the
top of a hovel, unique to
individual builders. This
hovel is at the Heron Cross
Pottery in Fenton, now
restored and incorporated
into a visitor centre*

The approach to construction was skilfully
casual, as was found at Piddinghoe in Sussex,
where the restoration of a kiln dating from around
1800 revealed that:

> *Whilst the work was skilfully executed in so far as
> the bricklayers knew exactly what they were about
> no time was spent in exactitudes or wasted on
> things that were not absolutely necessary. Angles,
> lines and levels varied to a considerable degree but
> have been adjusted to bring them back on to course
> by tricks of the trade.*[17]

It is said that the shape of the hovel depended
largely on the courage of the bricklayer, on his
confidence in pulling the brickwork over the
oven. A good degree of confidence resulted in a
full-bodied, 'burgundy' bottle shape; a lack of it
meant only a slightly tapered, 'hock' shape to the
hovel. Over-confidence resulted in the structure
falling in.[18] Many hovels had decorative brickwork
at the top, which was individual to the builder
(Plates 91, 92 and 93).

The shaping of the oven and its crown was
dependent equally on the skill of the bricklayer
and on how dry the fireclay mixture was in which
the bricks were laid. The bricklayer worked

parts sand and one part lime, which allowed for
expansion and contraction of the structure.[16]
Usually the oven had a double layer of bricks, the
hovel a single layer, and the brickwork was either
canted or stepped.

Plate 92
*Kilns at Minton Campbell
Pottery, Stoke-on-Trent*

round, staggering bricks on each course to allow for tightening up when it was complete. Both hovel and oven were scaffolded with timber on the inside, to provide platforms. The main bearing timbers were supported on ledges left in the brickwork. Platforms were then built around the perimeter, leaving a hole in the centre for materials to be carried up. When the whole was complete, the scaffolding was taken down one level at a time, and the holes filled in.[19]

Plate 93
Kilns at Taylor-Tunnicliffe's (formerly Hales, Hancock and Godwin), c1961

The up-draught oven continued to be used through to the present century. It usually had eight to eleven firemouths around the outside, depending on the size of the oven, with corresponding fireboxes inside. Flues ran underneath the floor, with a central well-hole and pipe-bung made up of open-ended saggars allowing heat up into the middle of the oven and smoke to escape. It is suggested that both the increase in number of firemouths and the provision of a central well-hole were modifications brought about by the transition from wood to coal-firing. The former was necessary because coal produced a build up of clinker in the firemouth which obstructed air flow into the oven: it is argued, therefore, that the problem was alleviated by constructing more firemouths.

Plate 94
Placing saggars in a kiln

However, the greater number of firemouths produced a considerable difference in temperature between the periphery and the centre of the oven, and led in turn to the introduction of the central flue and well-hole to help produce a more even spread of heat.[20] The entrance, or 'clammins', was bounded by an iron frame, and shaped for the passage of the ovenmen with saggars on their heads (Plate 94). It was sealed with bricks and clay before firing and broken open at the end. There were chain dampers to regulate heat, spy-holes to inspect the progress of the firing and trial holes through which to draw trials and the pyroscopes, or temperature gauges.

The capacity of the oven varied, with an average-sized oven holding around 2,000 saggars. These were stacked in bungs beginning at the far side of the oven, furthest from the entrance, and passing from the placers' heads to an ovenman on a horse or 'oss (ladder), in order to reach the top of the stacks. Different ware was placed in different parts of the oven, making use of the variation in temperature throughout the oven. The firing range was from around 1,000°C for biscuit firing, up to 1,260°C for stoneware glost firing. Depending on this, and on the size of oven, the complete cycle from placing to drawing the ware was from four to as many as fourteen days.[21]

While there is evidence of some wood-fired kilns for porcelain and enamelling during the mid eighteenth century (wood was preferable for the rapid, low-temperature firing of enamel decoration, and was less liable to pollute the pure porcelain colour in the kiln), the history of industrial pottery-making in the area is largely one of coal-fired pots. From the medieval period onwards, it seems that both charcoal and coal were used for firing by local potters, though the former probably declined as the sources were exhausted. A single firing used up to around twenty-seven tons of coal, which helps explain the importance of easy access to the fuel and space for a coal heap.[22] The quality of the coal was important. One with a high sulphur content produced damaging fumes, a coking one gave a sticky fuel, and one with a low ash fusibility would become a solid mass which was difficult to break up and take out at the end.[23]

The fireman played an extremely important role in the factory, for the success of the firing depended entirely on his knowledge and judgement. A fireman saw through the complete firing, sleeping in a cabin or shelter near to the kiln (Plate 95). Aside from the smoke, the heat created was enormous, and the extremes of temperature experienced by the oven workers in cold weather surpassed even those of the young mould runners with the stoves, since in many cases the former were operating between the furnace of the kiln and the open-air courtyard.

During the second half of the nineteenth century attempts were made to improve the design of the bottle oven, to give increased space and to distribute heat more evenly and effectively. The most successful was that of Thomas Minton in 1875–8, whose design dispensed with the old firemouths, which were set partly outside the oven and therefore expended the most heat in the surrounding brickwork. Instead, the combustion of the coal was effected entirely in the inside of the oven. In addition, a second chamber was placed on top of the oven, making use of heat escaping from the lower part to harden printed ware or for low-temperature firings. Such a

construction also obviated the need for a hovel, saving both money and space.[24]

The down-draught oven, developed in the early twentieth century to use heat more efficiently, was designed so that the heat rose and then was forced downwards through the setting, out through holes in the base of the oven, and the smoke rose through a straight chimney nearby. The advantages of this oven were that the draught and rate of fuel travel were steadier, that the honeycomb of underground flues helped heat up the dead part of the oven, that it produced a more uniform heat, and that it allowed the use of an inferior quality coal, since by this method all the products of combustion were consumed.[25]

Despite all these improvements, the efficiency of the coal-fired pot oven remained low. In a

Plate 95
The fireman. The iron bontings, which surrounded the oven structure and kept it stable during the continuous cycle of expansion and contraction, can clearly be seen in this view

series of tests in 1929, William Emery found that only a tiny amount of heat was used on the ware itself, the rest being lost in the surrounding structure and in combustion. His statistics were:

heat in ware	1.74%
saggars	9.60%
brickwork and radiation	36.36%
waste gases	52.30% [26]

The case for gas as a fuel was put forward in the early years of the century, on the grounds that it was clean, that it distributed temperature evenly, was quick to achieve its maximum temperature and reduced the destruction of the brickwork and saggars. It was estimated that between 175 and 200 saggars were destroyed in a coal-firing, as opposed to 40 in a gas-firing, which also indicates the deleterious effect on the oven brickwork.[27] The manufacturers were conservative in their choice of fuel as in all other areas of their factories. Coal was the traditional fuel, it was relatively cheap and was near at hand. In any case it may have been the general view, expressed by J Burton, Vice-President of the British Ceramic Society in 1906, that the improvements to fuel economy were over-emphasised: 'for in all pottery worthy of the name the quality of the ware should be the very first consideration – a high percentage of "best" being the chief point to aim at, and the cost of the fuel an item of secondary consideration'.[28] The bottle oven itself was an integral part of the potworks; it did not occupy a large space and could be erected in however irregular a spot on any potwork site. Thus, although tunnel ovens had been introduced in France as early as 1751 and became commonly used there in the nineteenth century, it is perhaps not surprising that it was not until 1912 that the first Dressler tunnel kiln was tried in the Potteries, first fired by coal, then by gas. At that time there were said to be over 1,200 bottle ovens in the area, and although the tunnel kiln gradually became a more common sight in the factories, it was not until the Clean Air Acts of 1960 that bottle ovens ceased operating, and the manufacturers were forced to turn to kilns fired by gas, oil or electricity.[29] During the intervening years, and more especially after 1960, the bottle ovens were demolished to make way for new tunnel kilns. These kilns in turn meant that completely new designs had to be drawn up for the whole factory, since they require long, open rooms in the body of the premises. Today, there are less than fifty pot ovens still standing, most of which are falling into decay.

The muffle kiln, used to fire decorated ware, was much smaller than the other types of kiln. It was of similar construction, but the flames were led around the muffle chamber by a series of flues and did not actually enter it, thereby protecting the delicate colours. The temperature required was lower than for biscuit firing, around 750–800°C. No saggars were necessary and nor was a hovel. Just as upper chambers were introduced into the ordinary bottle ovens, multi-chambered ovens came into use in this type also.

The calcining kilns, which are used in grinding mills to prepare mainly flint and bone, are a different type again. The burning or calcining is carried out to make the flint or bone brittle, and therefore easier to crush for use in pottery bodies. The kilns consist of a simple stack, with a bowl underneath to hold the raw material. Fire bars at the base of the bowl are removed to draw out the material at the end of firing. The flint is layered alternatively with fuel inside the

Plate 96
Wheatley's brick and tile works, Trent Vale

kiln, the fire is lit and the load left to burn for twenty-four to thirty-six hours. The capacity of surviving kilns varies from 15 to 40 tons, consuming from a half to one ton of fuel (now coke), and taken to a temperature of 900° to 1,000°C.[30]

Various types of kiln were used for firing bricks and tiles in England during the nineteenth century, but in the Potteries the round beehive kiln seems to have been the most common. In 1856 the engineer Humphrey Chamberlain wrote:

In Staffordshire, the bricks are burnt in small round kilns, called ovens, which hold from 7,000 to 8,000 bricks each; these are burnt from fire in the walls round the ovens, and the raw ware is set in, so as to form a flue from each fire, to direct the flame to the centre. These ovens burn very quickly, and a most intense heat can be obtained by them.[31]

The last few surviving beehive kilns in the Potteries at the Wheatley, Trent Vale, and Caddick Adams, Basford, works were recorded prior to their demolition in 1987–8 (Plates 96 and 97). Low, squat kilns, of similar circumference to bottle ovens, they worked on the down-draught principle and smoke was directed out by a separate chimney serving one or a group of kilns. Bricks and tiles were fired together, the former used as a bed for the tiles and to fill the gaps around the edge of the oven. They would burn for around thirty-six hours, consuming 3 to 4 tons of coal.[32]

The traditional brick kilns of the Potteries are an endangered group and very few now (1991) remain. Once the essential workhorses of the industry, they now stand idle in potwork yards, their role taken over by computer-operated kilns which quickly and efficiently fire the ware and give no sign to the outside world that the pottery industry is at work.

Plate 97
An aerial view of the Caddick Adams brick and tile works, Basford

GLOSSARY

ball clay
A very plastic secondary clay which burns white or cream. Thought to be so named from the shape of the pieces of clay made for ease of handling.

beehive oven
The type of oven in which bricks and tiles were traditionally fired in North Staffordshire, so named because of its low domed shape.

biscuit
Ware which has been fired once and is not yet glazed. A biscuit firing is the first firing.

blunging
The mixing of raw materials in water in preparation of a clay body.

body
Man-made mixture of clays and other materials, to produce particular qualities in a ware.

bonting
The iron band around the oven used to support the structure under the stress of expansion and contraction of the brickwork in heating and cooling the oven.

bottle oven
See **pot oven**.

bung
The column of saggars in a kiln. Also a stopper placed in the spy-hole of a kiln.

calcining
Making brittle by means of heating. Hard raw materials such as flint and bone are calcined before crushing. The heating also drives off combined water and organic impurities.

chert stone
A stone with a very high silica content.

clammins
The entrance to the oven which is sealed with bricks and clay before each firing.

dipping
Method of glaze application in which the ware is immersed in a tub of glaze.

down-draught
A type of kiln in which air rises up inside the oven to be forced back down and out through the base of the oven.

enamel
Metallic-based colour painted on to ware after the glost firing, and fired to a lower temperature of around 750° to 850°C.

encaustic
As a term applied to tiles, this refers to inlaid decoration. Plastic clay or slip, of a different colour to the original, is laid into the hollows of formed clay tiles.

fire bag
A small firebrick chimney above each firemouth on the inside of the oven, used to direct flames into the oven and to protect the nearby saggars.

firebox
The box structure, attached to the oven, which takes the coal.

fireclay
Clay able to withstand high temperatures and therefore used in kiln structures and furniture.

firemouth
The openings around the base of the oven in which fires are lit.

firing
The heating of ware in a kiln.

frit and frit kiln
Frit is part of a glaze which has been pre-melted, cooked and ground into a fine powder. This process renders water-soluble materials insoluble and lead compounds harmless, and achieves greater homogeneity of the glaze.

The frit kiln is the crucible-like furnace in which the melting takes place.

glaze
The glassy coating applied to pottery, in powder or liquid form.

glost
Glazed state. A glost firing is one in which glazed ware is being fired.

green ware
Clay ware before it has been fired.

handling
Fixing handles to ware.

hardening-on
Fixing underglaze colour by means of a low-temperature firing before the glost firing.

horse or 'oss
A wooden ladder used to reach the tops of the bungs of saggars in the oven.

hovel
The outer brick shell which encases and protects the oven.

jasper
A hard, fine, unglazed stoneware introduced by Josiah Wedgwood.

jigger
Mechanical methods for making flat ware, such as plates, from plastic clay. A slab of clay is placed on a solid plaster mould fixed to a turntable, the mould having the shape of the inside of the plate. A template fixed to a bar on a rigid frame is brought against the clay and the plate is formed by revolving the turntable.

jolley
Mechanical method for making hollow ware, such as cups, using the principle of mould and template. Here, the piece of clay is placed inside the hollow mould and the template lowered down on to it. The tool thus both presses the clay against the wall of the mould and shapes the inside of the vessel.

kiln
The structure, including oven and hovel, in which ware is fired. The tunnel kiln is the term used for the twentieth-century kiln of tunnel shape, into which trucks loaded with ware are drawn to be fired.

marl
Accurately, a secondary clay containing chalk. The term is also used to refer to low-quality fireclay which is used in making bricks and saggars.

muffle
Lining to a kiln designed to protect ware from the direct effect of flames.

oven
The inner structure in which ware is actually fired (the outer structure being the hovel).

pan
The vessel in which materials such as flint, bone and colours are ground.

paddle
The wooden implement used to stir slip in clay preparation.

placer and placing
The person and activity involved in setting ware in saggars or packing ware into a kiln.

pot oven
Term describing the entire kiln (both hovel and oven), used mainly up to the nineteenth century, before the kiln had become fully developed in shape.

The term 'bottle oven' arose from the full bottle shape of the hovel, which was developed during the eighteenth and nineteenth centuries. This term is still used today.

presser, pressing and press mould
The person and method involved in pressing clay into moulds as a way of making ware.

pug mill
Machine used for preparing clay in the plastic state.

saggar
Fireclay box in which ware is placed as a protection from the direct action of flames and gases during firing.

slip
Clay mixed with water to a creamy consistency.

slip-casting
A method of making ware by pouring slip into a plaster mould to form a thin wall of clay after which the excess slip is poured out of the mould.

smoke house
The room with the oven in which green ware is dried out.

stouker
Person who fixes handles to ware.

throwing
The method of making a pot by shaping plastic clay on a spinning turntable, known as a potter's wheel or throwing wheel.

tunnel kiln
See **kiln**.

turning
Completing the shape of a pot by paring down the sides and cutting the foot ring at the base. This is carried out when the pot is leather-hard, either on a lathe or inverted on a wheel.

up-draught
The type of oven and firing in which the air passes from the base of the kiln out through the top.

wedging
A method of preparing plastic clay by slamming and kneading a lump of clay in order to make its consistency even and to exclude air.

well-hole
The hole in the centre of the oven floor, over which baseless saggars are stacked. This forms a chimney and allows smoke to escape.

ABBREVIATIONS

BRL	Birmingham Central Reference Library, archive department
DL	Duchy of Lancaster
HBS	Historic Buildings Survey, Stoke-on-Trent City Museum and Art Gallery
HRL	Horace Barks Reference Library, Hanley
IAR	*Industrial Archaeology Review*
KUL	University of Keele Library, local collection
LJRO	Lichfield Joint Diocesan Record Office
NMR	National Monuments Record
NSFCT	*North Staffordshire Field Club Transactions*
NSJFS	*North Staffordshire Journal of Field Studies*
PRO	Public Record Office
RIBA	Royal Institute of British Architects
SAS	*Staffordshire Archaeological Studies*
SMAS	*Stoke-on-Trent City Museum and Art Gallery Archaeological Society Reports*
SRO	Staffordshire County Record Office, Stafford
STKMG	Stoke-on-Trent City Museum and Art Gallery
VCH	Victoria History of the Counties of England
WMS	Wedgwood manuscript, reference used in Wedgwood Collection, University of Keele Library

NOTES

INTRODUCTION

1 Pevsner 1974, p 252.
2 Foster 1908.

Chapter 1
POTTERY MANUFACTURE BEFORE 1700

1 For information on geology, coal and iron industries, see Beaver 1964, Hawke-Smith 1987, VCH 1967, *Staffs* vol II.
2 Mountford, Gee and Simpson 1968, p 19.
3 Middleton 1984, pp 41, 44.
4 Wedgwood 1924–5.
5 See *SMAS Reports* 3, 4, 6, 8, 10.
6 Plot 1686, p 122.
7 PRO DL30/240/8 1650–60.
8 SRO Aqualate MSS, Manor Court Records.
9 Weatherill 1971, p 139; author's research compiled from potters' inventories in Burslem, Hanley and Shelton, LJRO. This is a simplification of the argument; see Weatherill 1971 and 1981, and Nixon 1976, pp 12–14.
10 LJRO inventory Thomas Dakin, Shelton, 1680.
11 Nixon has found that there were different levels of involvement in the period between 1661 and 1740, ranging from potters with 'agricultural interests comparable with those of non-manufacturing farmers', to potters managing small farms, to those with no direct involvement in farming. Nixon 1976, p 13.
12 Plot 1686, p 123. The pot ovens shown in the illustration of the Churchyard Pottery are almost certainly nineteenth-century ones, as seen by the artist of the time.
13 LJRO inventory Raph Simpson, potter, Shelton, 1676.
14 LJRO inventory Samuel Simpson, Snape Marsh, 1703.
15 Weatherill 1971, p 61.

Chapter 2
THE DEVELOPMENT OF POTWORKS DURING THE EIGHTEENTH CENTURY

1 The accumulation of land by a number of individuals can be followed in the Manor Court Rolls, PRO DL30.
2 Ward 1843, p 46.
3 HRL Adams Collection EMT15/740A.
4 Ibid.
5 PRO DL30/507/15 1750.
6 PRO DL30/507/9 1734.
7 SRO D1788/P67/B22.
8 Ibid.
9 See Weatherill 1971 and 1981.
10 Weatherill 1971, p 61.
11 Ibid.
12 Ibid.
13 Bemrose 1972.
14 Tait and Cherry 1978, 1980.
15 Shaw 1829, p 155.
16 Mountford 1972, p 181.
17 See Nixon 1976, pp 203–5.
18 SRO D1788/P14/2
19 Guildhall Library, London, MS 11936, vol CL, p 338, insurance policy no. 20,4458.
20 SRO Baddeley Papers reproduced in Mallet 1966, 1967.
21 Job 1985, p 16.
22 See STKMG Heathcote Papers. Weatherill (1971, pp 64–5) believes the earliest date for specialised flint mills to be around 1726.
23 BRL Boulton and Watt portfolio 400.
24 VCH 1967, *Staffs* vol II, p 8; Copeland 1972, p 22.
25 SRO D1788/P1/1
26 For details of turnpike roads and canals, see Hawke-Smith 1985; VCH 1967, *Staffs* vol II; Thomas 1971.
27 Moisley 1951, p 154.
28 KUL WMS E25.18176.
29 KUL WMS E25.18198.
30 Wedgwood believed that John Brindley was at the head of an opposition against him in the battle for the canal route. KUL WMS E25.18198.
31 Aikin 1795, p 517. Also p 520, a similar description of Etruria. From certain documentary evidence it has been suggested that Wedgwood himself, under the alias of Aikin, wrote the part of the book referring to the Potteries, though if so the description of Etruria must have been written tongue-in-cheek.
32 DL private collection, memorandum concerning 1781 lease, from the 1777 survey of the Duchy of Lancaster estates.
33 KUL WMS, in Blake Roberts 1980, p 36.
34 A good account of the ramifications of the Lunar Circle is to be found in King-Hele 1977.
35 Jones 1985, pp 35–6.
36 Shaw 1829, p 190.
37 Meteyard 1865–6, vol I, fig 95.

38 KUL WMS E25.18184.
39 Ibid.
40 Ibid.
41 Ibid.
42 Archaeological excavation has revealed the range of Greatbatch's ware (1979–82 finds in collection of STKMG).
43 Meteyard 1865–6, vol II, p 495.
44 Ibid, p 496.
45 Weatherill 1981, pp 207, 210; KUL WMS E25.18197.
46 Barnard 1920.
47 Select Committee on the State of Children Employed in Manufactories of the United Kingdom, 1816, first examination of Josiah Wedgwood.
48 KUL WMS 4046.5.
49 Nichols 1931, p 53.
50 Markin 1985, pp 8–10.
51 Shaw 1829, p 30.
52 'A representation of the manufacturing of earthenware' 1827, a series of copper-plate engravings commissioned by Enoch Wood. British Ceramic Research Association.
53 Shaw 1829, p 166.
54 Ibid, p 119.
55 KUL WMS E25.18248.
56 KUL WMS E39.28409, Commonplace Book 1790–4, pp 7, 17.
57 KUL WMS E25.18248.
58 KUL WMS 4045.5, rules 6 and 7.
59 Original rope-pulley wheels are to be seen at the Stoke-on-Trent City Museum and Art Gallery and the Wedgwood Museum, Barlaston.
60 KUL WMS E25.18237.
61 Ward 1843, p 260.
62 KUL WMS E43.28642, an account of building and improvements on the Etruria estates, 1787.
63 Undated letter, late 1767 or early 1768, Darwin correspondence, quoted Meteyard 1865–6, vol II, p 30.
64 KUL WMS E25.18193.
65 Meteyard 1865–6, vol II, p 210.
66 Ibid, p 447.
67 KUL WMS 18587.25, 18660.25; also Evans 1970, p 247.
68 Thomas 1971, pp 44–5.
69 King-Hele 1977.
70 Thomas 1971, pp 46–8; BRL Boulton and Watt portfolio 96–7, Wedgwood correspondence.
71 BRL Boulton and Watt portfolio 218 reverse.
72 Barnard 1920, pp 6–14.
73 Ibid, p 12.
74 Copy of unidentified plan in the Stoke-on-Trent City Museum and Art Gallery, thought to be from KUL WMS.
75 KUL Spode MS 893, in Nixon 1976, p 116.
76 Minton archive, 1831–42, wages book.
77 For this and additional information on the Adams family, see Turner 1904.
78 VCH 1963, Staffs vol VIII, p 83.
79 Ibid, p 136.
80 Shaw 1829, p 30.
81 Markin 1984, p 20.
82 Winyard 1983.
83 Ibid.
84 KUL WMS E25.18191; KUL WMS E25.18199; KUL WMS E25.18206.
85 KUL WMS: see Winyard 1983, section 8.
86 Meteyard 1865–6, vol II, p 600.
87 Ibid, p 333n.
88 KUL WMS 1781–7. The young Flaxman was already designing ornamental plaques for chimney-pieces for Wedgwood's most well-to-do customers, including those made in 1777 for a chimney-piece at the nearby Longton Hall, being rebuilt by the same Thomas Gardner who had worked on Etruria.
89 Meteyard 1865–6, vol II, p 600.
90 Smiles 1894, p 206 n1.
91 KUL WMS D1785.
92 NMR BB75/3047.
93 Turner 1904, p 166.
94 Ward 1843, p 160.
95 Ibid, p 43.
96 There are numerous examples of conversion and division in the Manor Court Roll records of Hanley, Shelton and Penkhull, continuing into the nineteenth century with larger buildings and greater subdivision.
97 Copy of abstract of title Reverend Edward Whieldon 1809 in Morley-Hewitt 1954, pp 150–4. This includes cottages not connected with the manufactory.
98 Statistics drawn from the Guildhall Library, London, Sun Fire Insurance policies and Shropshire County Record Office, Shrewsbury, Salop Fire Office policy registers between the two dates.
99 Jewitt 1865, p 197.
100 Nixon 1976, p 200 (advertisement wrongly referenced).
101 Ward 1843, p 443.
102 VCH 1963, Staffs vol VIII, p 150.

Chapter 3
THE EARLY NINETEENTH CENTURY: SUCCESS AND EXPANSION

1 Allbut 1802.
2 STKMG Enoch Wood Scrapbook 1, items 226–44.
3 Ward 1843, p 43.
4 Monthly Magazine, 1 November 1823.

5 KUL Sneyd Papers, 1720.

6 LJRO Tithe Survey, Tunstall.

7 The complete history of Mare's acquisition of the land and sale to individual purchasers can be followed in the Manor Court Rolls, PRO DL30. Notes from these available in STKMG archive.

8 This was the scheme initiated by Valentine Close, potter and flint-grinder, who bought the land for development and sold it off over a number of years. Plan dated 1806 in DL private collection, details of transactions in Manor Court Rolls PRO DL30. Copies of both in STKMG archive.

9 The clubs included those of Thistley Field (1797), Haynes Meadow (1801), Hill Street (1801), John Street (1805) and Hanley and Shelton Independent (1808). Details on these in PRO DL30, with plans in DL private collection.

10 PRO DL30/507/26 onward. Includes plan. Copies of transactions and plan in STKMG archive.

11 Shaw 1829, pp 72–3.

12 *Staffordshire Advertiser*, 19 April 1806. A horse-drawn tram appears on the illustration of Enoch Wood's Fountain Place Pottery.

13 Ibid, 14 November 1801.

14 Ibid, 19 September 1818.

15 *Monthly Magazine*, 1 November 1823.

16 HBS S140.

17 Shaw 1829, p 63.

18 Ibid, p 77.

19 Anon 1848, p 33; VCH 1963, *Staffs* vol VIII, p 114.

20 The detailed information from which these statistics are drawn has been found in the Manor Court Rolls, PRO DL30 (see above, note 9).

21 See notes 9 and 20. Other sources on building clubs during this period include land-tax returns, insurance policies, newspaper advertisements and original society booklets in the William Salt Library, Stafford.

22 HBS T122 and T200; Tunstall Building Society Articles of Agreement 1816, William Salt Library, Stafford.

23 Parliamentary Debates, House of Commons, 10 April 1818.

24 Children's Employment Commission 1842, report by Samuel Scriven C2.

25 Select Committee on the State of Children Employed in the Manufactories of the United Kingdom, first examination of Josiah Wedgwood.

26 Shaw 1829, p 161.

27 Shropshire County Record Office, Shrewsbury, Salop Fire Office policy 11283, 2 December 1816, Miles Mason, Lane Delph. See the Guildhall Library, London, Sun Fire Insurance policy registers and Shropshire County Record Office, Shrewsbury, Salop Fire Office registers for entries of potters 1763–1816.

28 Shropshire County Record Office, Shrewsbury, Salop Fire Office policy 2391, 16 July 1802, William Mellor (note added in 1806).

29 Jones 1985, p 45; Fitzgerald 1988, p 128.

30 KUL WMS 19963.28.

31 Shaw 1829, p 70.

32 Nixon 1976, p 176.

33 *Art Union*, 1 November 1846, p 289.

34 Shaw 1903, pp 47–8.

35 BRL Boulton and Watt portfolio 430.

36 Factories Inquiry Commission 1833, p 78.

37 See Burchill and Ross 1977.

38 HBS H158.

39 *Staffordshire Advertiser*, 7 November 1801 and 27 February 1802.

40 Factories Inquiry Commission 1833, p 79.

41 It is difficult to determine from Hargreaves 1832; present on Homer 1857.

42 Children's Employment Commission 1842, statement no. 93 Thomas Furnival.

43 *Staffordshire Advertiser*, 18 March 1815.

44 Children's Employment Commission 1842, statement no. 88 Hannah Fenton.

45 Ibid, statement no. 89 Thomas Baker.

46 *Staffordshire Advertiser*, 14 March 1829.

47 HBS L159.

48 SRO D593/11/14/3/62; D593/9/2/5/3; D593/H/3/39A.

49 STKMG Meigh transcript from the Rate Books; SRO D593/9/2/5/3.

50 HBS F139; STKMG Meigh transcript from the Rate Books. For schedule of the pottery, see SRO D3272/1/17/1/80.

51 Shaw 1829, p 69.

52 Ward 1843, p 553.

53 Shaw 1829, p 71.

54 Ibid, pp 71–2; Jewitt 1878, p 411.

55 Children's Employment Commission 1842, report no. 293.

56 Hargreaves 1832; 1849 tithe map for Fenton.

57 Ure 1839, p 1021.

Chapter 4
THE MID NINETEENTH CENTURY: THE PRICE OF INDUSTRIALISATION

1 White 1851; Thomas 1971, p 13.

2 Shaw 1903, p 124.

3 Anon 1848, pp 42–3.

4 Shaw 1903, p 187.

5 *Staffordshire Advertiser*, 2 June 1849, in Nixon 1976, p 196.

6 VCH 1963, *Staffs* vol VIII, p 135; National Society for Promoting Education Archive, St John's, Goldenhill; Pevsner 1974, pp 206–65.

7 Children's Employment Commission 1842, report by Samuel Scriven.

8 Ibid, statement nos 179, 193, 291, 55.

9 Ibid, statement no. 35.

10 Ibid, report by Samuel Scriven.

11 Factory Inspectorate 1865, reports of the Inspectors of Factories, 31 January 1865, p 60.

12 Ibid, p 57.

13 Ibid, p 59.

14 Ibid, p 62.

15 Children's Employment Commission 1862, summary report by Mr Longe.

16 Children's Employment Commission 1842, statement no. 49.

17 Haggar and Adams 1977, p 94.

18 Evans 1846, pp 22–30.

19 Factory Inspectorate 1865, reports of the Inspectors of Factories 31 January 1865, p 53.

20 Shaw 1903, p 185.

21 Ibid, p 187.

22 KUL British Parliamentary Papers, House of Commons debate 14 June 1864, Factory Acts Extension Bill.

23 Children's Employment Commission 1862, Memorial of Employers in the Potteries, 1st report of the Commissioners, p 322.

24 Children's Employment Commission 1862, evidence of William Moore.

25 Factory Inspectorate 1865, reports of the Inspectors of Factories 31 October 1865, p 102.

26 Factory Inspectorate 1865, reports of the Inspectors of Factories 31 January 1865, p 68.

27 Factory Inspectorate 1867, reports of the Inspectors of Factories 30 April 1867, p 24.

28 KUL British Parliamentary Papers 1871, vol LXII, p 146.

29 *Staffordshire Advertiser*, 10 February 1866.

30 Factory Inspectorate 1865, reports of the Inspectors of Factories 31 January 1865, p 60.

31 HBS L206; title deeds and other legal documents in possession of Aynsley China Ltd.

32 Children's Employment Commission 1862, evidence of John Aynsley.

33 HBS S190.

34 STKMG exhibition catalogue 'Minton tiles 1835–1935'.

35 See Austwick and Austwick 1980; *The Builder*, 27 March 1869.

36 *The Builder*, 27 March 1869.

37 McCarthy 1875–80, p 73.

38 Jewitt 1878, p 397.

39 Dobson 1850, pp 97, 101.

40 Chamberlain 1856.

41 HBS S143.

42 Information from Mr E Mountford, fitter, employee of the Wheatley Works.

43 White 1851.

44 Green *et al* 1986; Lambert 1865, pp 42–6.

45 HBS S123, S128; Minutes of the Stokeville Building Society; Turner nd.

46 HBS L213, title deeds.

47 HRL, 1851 Census.

48 Stanley 1845, p 211.

49 Lee 1850; Ranger 1854; Rawlinson 1850; Reports to the General Board of Health.

50 PRO MH12/11470. Dr Ballard's report 1872, Longton; MH12/11499, Medical Officer annual report 1892, Stoke-on-Trent.

51 PRO MH12/11470. Dr Ballard's report 1872, Stoke.

52 For freehold land societies, see HBS F106, F163; also Gallimore 1984; Botham 1972. The contribution of the Duke of Sutherland in Dresden, Florence and Normacot can be followed in the records of the Sutherland MSS, SRO; also Longton 1883; Briggs 1982; VCH 1963, *Staffs* vol VIII, p 227.

53 Burnett 1978, p 169.

54 HBS F110. There are attractive Gothic cottages of yellow brick at Foundry Square, Norton, HBS B189.

55 See HBS H193.

56 Shaw 1829, p 62.

57 HBS S165, S173, S179, S180, S185.

58 RIBA ScGGS/4/8/1.

59 Caffyn 1986, pp 58–63.

60 *Staffordshire Advertiser*, 2 February 1856.

61 HRL, 1861 Census.

62 *Staffordshire Sentinel*, 2 February 1856; obituary of Herbert Minton, *The Times*, 8 April 1858.

63 PRO DL30/507/72.

Chapter 5
THE LATER NINETEENTH CENTURY: ECONOMY AND RENEWAL

1 Lamb 1977, p 59.

2 *The Furniture Gazette*, 3 April 1875.

3 *The Staffordshire Times*, 22 July 1876. The architect of the alterations was Robert Scrivener.

4 KUL British Parliamentary Papers, US Consul Report, 49 Congress 1 Session, House of Representatives Miscellaneous Document 24.

5 Lamb 1977, p 60.

6 For these and other factories, see Anon nd, *c*1893.

7 Architects listed in local trade directories for this period.

8 Anon nd, *c*1893, p 74.

9 Ibid, p 21.

10 See *The Building News*, April to November 1896.

11 For a detailed description of machinery, see Celoria 1973, pp 11–48.

12 See Factory Inspectorate 1865, reports of the Inspectors of Factories 31 January 1865, Robert Baker, p 55. To some extent the comparative space available to particular groups of workers in the factory can be found from the number of people in the different areas.

13 Hatton 1898, pp 30–1. In some of the older factories even the artist élite was in cramped quarters, eg, the Minton factory as reported in the *Pottery Gazette Supplement*, 1 December 1883.

14 KUL British Parliamentary Papers, 1893–4, vol XVII, p 8.

15 Bennett 1902, p 48.

16 Ibid, p 115.

17 Hatton 1898, pp 29–44.

18 HBS B203; History of the firm in Burgess and Leigh Ltd, nd.

19 Anon nd, *c*1893, p 57.

20 Ibid, p 58.

21 *Pottery Gazette Supplement*, 1 December 1883.

22 HBS S145; Stoke Rate Books.

23 HBS H104; Hanley Rate Books.

24 Stuart 1985.

25 VCH 1963, *Staffs* vol VIII, pp 81, 107, 144, 227.

26 PRO MH12/11470 Dr Ballard's report.

27 VCH 1963, *Staffs* vol VIII, pp 210, 224.

Chapter 6
THE EARLY TWENTIETH CENTURY: FUNCTIONALISM AND BEYOND

1 See HBS file Penkhull Garden Village.

2 Stoke-on-Trent Tenants Ltd *c*1913.

3 *Staffordshire Weekly Sentinel*, 23 May 1919, dinner speech at Stoke Working Men's Club.

4 See Stoke-on-Trent City Council minutes 1919–22; Staffordshire Weekly Sentinel 1919–25; Stoke-on-Trent Housing Committee 1960, local government pamphlet.

5 *Staffordshire Weekly Sentinel*, 4 September 1925.

6 See HBS L203, L204, L205.

7 Stoke-on-Trent Council minutes, 4 May 1922; *Staffordshire Weekly Sentinel*, 19 July 1921.

8 'The pottery industry 1900–24', unpublished lecture by R Whipp presented to seminar at University of Keele for study of local and community history, March 1983.

9 *Pottery Gazette*, 1 December 1914, p 1387.

10 HBS S117, S118.

11 *Pottery Gazette*, 1 May 1920, p 650.

12 HBS B199; family records and assistance from Miss B Moorcroft and Mr W Moorcroft; Atterbury 1973.

13 *Pottery Gazette*, 1 October 1913, p 1147.

14 Burton 1913, p 78.

15 The firm began production there in 1940, though the war interrupted completion of the factory. Production continued at Etruria until 1950. Kelly 1975, pp 64–6.

Appendix
THE POT OVEN

1 Middleton 1984, pp 41–4.

2 Plot 1686, p 123.

3 SRO D1788/P33/B1.

4 Celoria and Kelly 1973; Greaves and Kelly 1974.

5 SRO D1788/P61/B41.

6 Parson and Bradshaw 1818, p *xlvi*. Salt-glazing was an important feature of the early pottery industry, and ideally required a separate kiln since the chemical reaction of the salt deposits in the kiln contaminated future ware.

7 SRO D1788/P33/B1.

8 British Patent Office, patent no. 83, 1635.

9 Meteyard 1865–6, vol II, pp 468–71.

10 Smiles 1894, p 243.

11 KUL WMS E25.18171.

12 Shaw 1829, p 152.

13 KUL WMS E25.18182.

14 Evans 1846, p 32.

15 Building specification courtesy of Miss B Moorcroft, copy with HBS B199.

16 Information from James Birks, Fenton; see HBS pot-oven survey.

17 O'Shea 1982, p 5.

18 Information from James Birks, Fenton; see HBS pot-oven survey.

19 Ibid.

20 Nixon 1976, pp 134–44.

21 Ibid, p 150.

22 Ibid, pp 52–4.

23 Hind 1937, pp 52–4.

24 Minton Museum, MSS and plans.

25 *Transactions British Ceramic Society* 1915–16, **15**, p 73.

26 Fox 1939; Hind 1937, p 70.

27 Murray 1907, pp 21, 28–9.

28 Burton 1906, p 122.

29 Ibid; Dinsdale 1953, p 373.

30 STKMG flint-kiln survey, Archaeology Department.

31 Chamberlain 1856, p 13.

32 Dobson 1850, p 101.

BIBLIOGRAPHY AND FURTHER READING

The historical records of Stoke-on-Trent are scattered throughout the country, making any comprehensive research a lengthy and at times frustrating task. There are numerous local collections aside from the Horace Barks Reference Library and the Staffordshire County Record Office (which provide useful material on the pottery industry), of which the most valuable is the extensive Wedgwood collection held at the University of Keele. The Historic Buildings Survey archive at the Stoke-on-Trent City Museum and Art Gallery is an important starting point for any study of local architecture, as it includes not only pottery factories and housing but also public buildings, schools, workhouses and other building types in the Potteries.

Further afield, the most useful source for studying the development of the pottery factories, housing and urban centres is the Duchy of Lancaster collection relating to Hanley, Shelton, Stoke-on-Trent and Penkhull within the Manor of Newcastle under Lyme. Of these, the Manor Court Rolls are held in the Public Record Office, Chancery Lane, while plans belonging to particular areas and properties are in the private collection of the Duchy of Lancaster in London. Copies of the most important of these are now available in the Historic Buildings Survey archive. The Poor Law Union Papers at the Public Record Office, Kew, contain valuable information on environmental and living conditions in the nineteenth-century Potteries, as well as details on all public buildings (including the art schools) and works requiring government loans.

ARCHIVAL SOURCES

Birmingham Central Reference Library, archives
Boulton and Watt MSS (portfolios of engine and mill drawings, Josiah Wedgwood, Josiah Spode, Robert Hamilton)

British Patent Office
British patent number 83, 1635, pottery kiln

Guildhall Library, London
Sun Fire Insurance policy registers 1763–1813

Horace Barks Reference Library, Hanley
Adams Collection (thought to have been assembled by P W L Adams for her *History of the Adams Family*, 1914. Relates to property, including potworks, in North Staffordshire, eighteenth and nineteenth centuries)

General Register Office, 1841, 1851, 1861 Census of Great Britain: North Staffordshire

Hanley Rate Books 1878–1900

Stoke-on-Trent City Council minutes of meetings 1919–22

University of Keele Library, local collection
Sneyd MSS (rentals, memos, development proposals in Tunstall and Burslem, eighteenth and nineteenth centuries)

Spode MSS (includes insurance plans, nineteenth century)

Warrillow Collection of photographs, nineteenth and twentieth centuries

Wedgwood MSS (correspondence, ledgers, plans, documents, eighteenth and nineteenth centuries)

Lichfield Joint Diocesan Record Office
Inventories and wills, seventeenth and eighteenth centuries

Tithe Survey (apportionments 1837–51; tithe redemption certificates 1828–73)

Minton Museum, Stoke
Minton kiln patent and drawings

Photographs and plans of factories relating to Hartshill and the Minton Memorial Building

National Society for Promoting Religious Education Archive, London
St John's C E School, Goldenhill, file nineteenth century

Public Record Office, Chancery Lane, London
Duchy of Lancaster, Newcastle under Lyme Manor Court Rolls 1650–60; 1730–1860

Public Record Office, Kew

Poor Law Union Papers:
   MH12/11203 Wolstanton 415 1871–2
   MH12/11229 Wolstanton 415 1893–6
   MH12/11470 Stoke-on-Trent 425 1871–2
   MH12/11471 Stoke-on-Trent 425 1873
   MH12/11499 Stoke-on-Trent 1893–6
   MH12/11503 Stoke-on-Trent 425 1893–6

Education papers:
   ED29/129 Wedgwood Memorial Institute
   ED29/132 Hanley British Schools
   ED29/134 Sutherland Institute
   ED29/137 Minton Memorial Building
   ED29/138 Jubilee Buildings

Shropshire County Record Office, Shrewsbury

Salop Fire Office policy registers 1786–1825

Staffordshire County Record Office, Stafford

Aqualate MSS (legal documents concerning potworks and potters)

Land tax returns 1826, 1831

Marquis of Stafford's plan for housing development in Longton 1824 D593/H144a–d

Memorial of the copyholders of Hanley and Shelton to his Grace the Duke of Sutherland 1840 D593/B1/14/26

Sutherland MSS (a large collection including legal documents, plans and details on development in the Longton area of the Sutherland estate)

Stoke-on-Trent City Museum and Art Gallery, Hanley

Exhibition catalogue 'Minton tiles 1835–1935'

Historic Buildings Survey archive (a comprehensive archive relating to buildings in Stoke-on-Trent. Includes a card index record with photographs of all pre-1924 buildings in the City, also a more detailed record of over 200 buildings, consisting of architectural drawings, photographs and historical abstracts)

Meigh, A (a transcription of the rate and assessment upon land and buildings within the parish of Stoke-on-Trent, 1807–59)

Donald Morris photographic collection of local buildings and the pottery industry

Whieldon notebook (archive of mainly legal documents relating to various estates in the Potteries, including the Whieldon estate, eighteenth and nineteenth centuries)

Enoch Wood Scrapbook

Other sources

The Minutes of the Stokeville Building Society, 1850–86. In the possession of the Honorary Secretary to the Villas Residents Committee, Mr Anthony Poole

Royal Institute of British Architects, letter from George Gilbert Scott to the Revd E Boyce, 31 December 1841, ScGGS/4/8/1

PRINTED SOURCES

Adams, P W L 1914. *A History of the Adams Family of North Staffordshire*. St Catherine Press, London

Aikin, J 1795. *A Description of the Country from Thirty to Forty Miles Round Manchester*. London

Allbut, T 1800. *View of the Staffordshire Potteries*. Burslem

1802. *The Staffordshire Pottery Directory*. Burslem

Anon 1848. *The Land We Live In*. Charles Knight

Anon nd, *c*1893. *A Descriptive Account of the Potteries*. Robinson, Son and Pike, Brighton

Arlidge, J T 1892. *The Pottery Manufacture in its Sanitary Aspects*

Art Union, 1 November 1846

Aslin, E and Atterbury, P 1976. *Minton 1798–1910*. Victoria and Albert Museum Exhibition Catalogue. HMSO, London

Atterbury, P 1973. *William Moorcroft and Walter Moorcroft*. Fine Art Society Exhibition Catalogue. R Dennis, London

Austwick, J and Austwick, B 1980. *The Decorated Tile: an Illustrated History of English Tile Making and Design*. Pitman House, London

Barnard, H 1920. *Artes Etruriae Renascuntur*. A record of the historical old pottery works of Messrs Josiah Wedgwood & Sons Ltd, Etruria, England

Barnett, H and Phillips, J 1987. *Suburban Style – The British Home 1840–1960*. Macdonald Orbis, London

Beaver, S H 1964. The Potteries: a study in the evolution of a cultural landscape. Presidential address delivered to the Institute of British Geographers

Bemrose, P J 1972. Newcastle under Lyme: its contribution to the growth of the North Staffordshire pottery industry 1650–1800. Unpublished MA thesis, University of Keele

Bennett, A 1902. *Anna of the Five Towns*. Methuen, London. Reprinted 1988, Penguin, Harmondsworth

—— 1910. *Clayhanger*. Reprinted 1985, Penguin, Harmondsworth

Beresford, M W 1971. The back-to-back house in Leeds, 1787–1837. In *The History of Working-class Housing: a Symposium*, ed S D Chapman, pp 93–132. David and Charles, Newton Abbot

Blake Roberts, G 1980. The architecture of Etruria and Barlaston. In *Wedgwood of Etruria and Barlaston*, ed K Niblett, pp 35–41. STKMG Exhibition Catalogue

Botham, F W 1972. Working-class housing in the North Staffordshire Potteries 1760–1910. Unpublished BA thesis, University of Nottingham

Briggs, J 1982. *A History of Longton*. Department of Adult Education, University of Keele

Brockman, H A N 1974. *The British Architect in Industry 1841–1940*. Allen and Unwin, London

Builder, The, 1869, 1878

Building News, The 1896. Series of articles on the Factory and Workshop Acts, April to November

Burchill, F and Ross, R 1977. *A History of the Potters' Union*. Ceramic and Allied Trades Union, Stoke-on-Trent

Burgess and Leigh Ltd nd. *A Century of Progress 1851–1951*

Burnett, J 1978. *A Social History of Housing 1815–1970*. Methuen, London

Burslem 1807. *Articles of the Burslem United and Amicable Building Company*. William Salt Library, Stafford

Burton, J 1906. The principles of the construction and firing of potters' ovens and kilns. *Transactions British Ceramic Society* **5**, 122–49

Burton, W 1913. *An Analysis of the Regulations Governing the Manufacture of Pottery in the British Isles*. Publication of the *Pottery Gazette*

Caffyn, L 1986. *Workers' Housing in West Yorkshire 1750–1920*. West Yorkshire Metropolitan County Council and Royal Commission on the Historical Monuments of England, HMSO, London

Celoria, F 1973. Ceramic machinery of the nineteenth century in the Potteries and other parts of Britain. *Staffordshire Archaeology* **2**, 11–48

—— 1983. Working and living conditions of nineteenth-century potters in Staffordshire. In *Staffordshire Porcelain*, ed G Godden. Granada, St Albans

Celoria, F and Kelly, J 1973. A post-medieval site with a kiln base found off Albion Square, Hanley, Stoke-on-Trent. *SMAS* **4**

Chalkin, C W and Havingden, M A (eds) 1974. *Rural Change and Urban Growth 1500–1800*. Longman, London

Chamberlain, H 1856. *Brickworking*. London

Children's Employment Commission 1842. Appendix to the second report of the Commissioners, trades and manufactures. Vol II: reports and evidence from sub-commissioners. HMSO, London 1842

—— 1862. First report of the Commissioners, section 1, 'The pottery manufacture', with an appendix of the reports and evidence of the Assistant Commissioners 1862, and memorial of employers in the Potteries. HMSO, London 1863

Copeland, R 1972. *Cheddleton Flint Mill and the History of Pottery Milling, 1726–1900*. Cheddleton Flint Mill Industrial Heritage Trust, Cheddleton

Cruickshank, D 1985. *A Guide to the Georgian Buildings of Britain and Ireland*. The National Trust and the Georgian Society, Weidenfield and Nicolson, London

Dinsdale, A 1953. The development of firing in the pottery industry. In *Ceramics: a Symposium*, ed A Green and G Stewart, pp 363–97. British Ceramic Society, Stoke-on-Trent

Dobson, E 1850. *A Rudimentary Treatise on the Manufacture of Brick and Tiles; Containing an Outline of the Principles of Brickmaking*. Reprinted in *Journal of Ceramic History* (1971) **5** (whole volume)

Dudson, A 1985. *Dudson. A Family of Potters Since 1800*. Dudson Publications, Stoke-on-Trent

Evans, H 1970. Wedgwood, windmills and water power. *Proceedings of the Wedgwood Society* **8**, 243–51

Evans, W 1846. *Art and History of the Potting Business*. Reprinted in *Journal of Ceramic History* (1970) **3**, 21–43

Evening Sentinel, 1900, 1907

Factories Inquiry Commission 1833. *First report of the Control Board of His Majesty's Commissioners appointed to collect information of children in factories...with minutes of evidence and reports by the district commissioners*. 28 June 1833. Reprinted 1968, F Cass and Co, London

Factory Inspectorate 1865. *Reports of the Inspectors of Factories to Her Majesty's Principal Secretary of State for the Home Department. Half-year ending 31 October 1864*. HMSO, London 1865

1865. *Reports of the Inspectors of Factories to Her Majesty's Principal Secretary of State for the Home Department. Half-year ending 30 April 1865*. HMSO, London 1865

1865. *Reports of the Inspectors of Factories to Her Majesty's Principal Secretary of State for the Home Department. Half-year ending 31 October 1865*. HMSO, London 1866

1866. *Reports of the Inspectors of Factories to Her Majesty's Principal Secretary of State for the Home Department. Half-year ending 30 April 1866*. HMSO, London 1866

1867. *Reports of the Inspectors of Factories to Her Majesty's Principal Secretary of State for the Home Department. Half-year ending 31 October 1866*. HMSO, London 1867

Fitzgerald, R 1988. The development of the cast-iron frame in textile mills to 1850. *IAR* **10** (2), 127–45

Foster, J F 1908. *Life's Contrasts: the Tragedy of the Potteries*. HRL

Fox, J 1939. Some factors influencing the choice of fuels in kilns in the ceramic industries. Uncorrected advance copy of a paper to be presented to the members of the Institute of Fuel, Geological Society, Burlington House, Piccadilly, 23 March 1939

Furniture Gazette 1875. Messrs Bates, Elliot and Co's works, Burslem 3 April. Reprinted in Local History Pamphlet 27, HRL

Galbraith, F nd. Bottle-oven survey. Unpublished survey, copy in STKMG

Gallimore, P 1984. Building societies and housing provision in North Staffordshire (1850–1880). 2 vols. Unpublished MA thesis, University of Keele

Gauldie, E 1974. *Cruel Habitations: a History of Working-class Housing 1780–1914*. Allen and Unwin, London

Greaves, S J and Kelly, J H 1974. The excavation of a kiln base in Old Hall Street, Hanley. *SMAS* **6**

Green, T *et al* 1986. Jesse Shirley's bone and flint mill, Stoke-on-Trent. *IAR* **9** (1), 57–70

Haggar, R G 1953. *A Century of Art Education in the Potteries*. R G Haggar, Stoke-on-Trent

Haggar, R G and Adams, E 1977. *Mason Porcelain and Ironstone 1796–1853*. Faber and Faber, London

Hampson, R 1986. The development of the pottery industry in Longton 1700–1865. Unpublished MA thesis, University of Keele

Harrison, T W 1902. *Municipal Dwellings for the Very Poor. A Scheme for Dealing with the Slum Districts of Hanley, Stoke-on-Trent*. Reprinted in Local History Pamphlet 38, HRL

Hatton, J 1898. *Twyfords. A Chapter in the History of Pottery*. J S Virtue & Co Ltd, London

Hawke-Smith, C 1985. *The Making of the Six Towns*. STKMG publication

1987. The Potteries landscape 1500–1820. *SAS* **4** 94–124

Hind, S R 1937. *Contributions to the Study of Pottery Ovens, Fuels and Firing*. British Pottery Manufacturers' Federation, Stoke-on-Trent

Hole, J 1866. *The Houses of the Working Classes with Suggestions for Their Improvement*. London

Jewitt, L 1865. *The Wedgwoods: Being a Life of Josiah Wedgwood*. J S Virtue & Co Ltd, London

1878. *The Ceramic Art of Great Britain*. J S Virtue & Co Ltd, London; revised edition by G Godden, *Jewitt's Ceramic Art of Great Britain 1800–1900*, Barrie and Jenkins, London 1972

Job, B 1985. *Staffordshire Windmills.* Midland Wind and Watermills Group, Birmingham

Jones, E 1985. *Industrial Architecture in Britain 1750–1939.* Batsford, London

Keates 1879. *Gazetteer and Directory of the Potteries and Newcastle under Lyme.* Hanley.

Kelly, A 1975. *The Story of Wedgwood.* Faber and Faber, London

King-Hele, D 1977. *Doctor of Revolution: the Life and Genius of Erasmus Darwin.* Faber and Faber, London

(ed) 1981. *The Letters of Erasmus Darwin.* Cambridge University Press, Cambridge

Kohl, J G 1845. *Travels in England and Wales*

Lamb, A 1977. Mechanisation and the application of steam power in the North Staffordshire pottery industry 1793–1914. *NSJFS* **17**, 50–64

Lambert, G 1865. *Art céramique. Description de la fabrication actuelle des faïences fines et autres poteries en Angleterre.* Brussels

Lee, W 1850. *Report to the General Board of Health on a Preliminary Inquiry into the Sewerage, Drainage and Supply of Water, and the Sanitary Condition of the Inhabitants of the Parish of Burslem.* HMSO, London

Longton 1883. Longton Borough Extension and Improvement Bill. Select Committee 1883, minutes of evidence (HRL S840/352/05)

Mallet, J 1966. John Baddeley of Shelton. Part 1. *Transactions of the English Ceramic Circle* **6** (2), 124–66

1967. John Baddeley of Shelton. Part 2. *Transactions of the English Ceramic Circle* **6** (3), 181–247

Markin, T 1983. Thomas Wolfe and his associates. Part 1. *Northern Ceramic Society Newsletter* **52**, 21–9

1984. Thomas Wolfe and his associates. Part 2. *Northern Ceramic Society Newsletter* **55**, 15–22

1985. Thomas Wolfe: man of property. Part 3. *Northern Ceramic Society Newsletter* **58**, 6–15

McCarthy, J F *c*1875–1880. *Great Industries of Great Britain*, vol III

McKendrick, N 1961. Josiah Wedgwood and factory discipline. *Historical Journal* **4** (1), 30–55

Meteyard, E 1865–6. *The Life of Josiah Wedgwood,* vols I and II. Hurst and Blackett, London; reprinted Josiah Wedgwood and Sons Ltd, Barlaston 1970

Middleton, S 1984. The Sneyd Green medieval kilns. *SAS* **1**, 41–7

Moisley, H A 1951. The industrial and urban development of the North Staffordshire conurbation. *Transactions and Papers, Institute of British Geographers* **17**, 151–65

Monthly Magazine, 1 November 1823. Article cutting from magazine in Broughton's 'Staffordshire Collections' book of cuttings, WSL PN4246/73

Morley-Hewitt, A 1954. Early Whieldon of the Fenton Low Works. *Transactions of the English Ceramic Circle* **3**, 142–54

Mountford, A R 1972. Thomas Whieldon's manufactory at Fenton Vivian. *Transactions of the English Ceramic Circle* **8** (2), 164–82

Mountford, A R, Gee, J and Simpson, G 1968. The excavation of an early Neronian pottery-kiln and workshop at Trent Vale, Stoke-on-Trent. *NSJFS* **8**, 19–38

Murray, W F 1907. The pottery oven of the future. *Transactions of the British Ceramic Society* **6**, 13–42

Muthesius, S 1982. *The English Terraced House.* Yale University Press, New Haven and London

Nichols, R 1931. *Ten Generations of a Potting Family.* Lund Humphries & Co Ltd, London

Nixon, M 1976. The emergence of the factory system in the Staffordshire pottery industry. Unpublished DPhil thesis, University of Aston in Birmingham

O'Shea, E W 1982. Restoration of a tile kiln at Piddinghoe. *Sussex Industrial History* **12**, 2–245

Parker, R B and Unwin, R 1901. *The Art of Building a Home.* Longman, London

Parliamentary Debates, 27 January–13 April 1818, 37. Hansard, London

Parson, W and Bradshaw, T 1818. *Staffordshire General and Commercial Directory,* Part 1

Penny Magazine, The 1843. A day at the Staffordshire Potteries. May Supplement, **12**, no. 716

Pevsner, N 1974. *The Buildings of England: Staffordshire.* Penguin, Harmondsworth

Pitt, W A 1817. *A Topographical History of Staffordshire.* Newcastle under Lyme

Plot, R 1686. *The Natural History of Staffordshire.* Oxford

Pottery Gazette, 1882, 1883, 1914, 1920

Priestley, J 1934. *English Journey.* Heinemann, London. Reprinted 1977, Penguin, Harmondsworth

Ranger, W 1854. *Report to the General Board of Health on a Preliminary Inquiry into the Sewerage, Drainage and Supply of Water, and the Sanitary Condition of the Inhabitants of the Township of Tunstall.* HMSO, London 1855

Rawlinson, R 1850. *Report to the General Board of Health on a Preliminary Inquiry into the Sewerage, Drainage and Supply of Water, and the Sanitary Condition of the Inhabitants of the Towns and Districts of Hanley and Shelton, Stoke, Fenton and Longton.* HMSO, London

Roberts, J 1983. *Working-class Housing in Nineteenth-century Manchester.* Neil Richardson, Manchester

Shaw, C 1903. *When I was a Child.* Reprinted 1977, Caliban, Sussex

Shaw, S 1829. *History of the Staffordshire Potteries.* Reprinted 1970, David and Charles, Newton Abbot, and S R Publishers, Wakefield

Skinner, D and Van Lemmen, H 1984. *Minton Tiles 1835–1935.* STKMG Exhibition Catalogue

Smiles, S 1894. *Josiah Wedgwood, His Personal History.* John Murray, London

Smith, D M 1965. Industrial architecture in the Potteries. *NSJFS* **5**, 81–94

Staffordshire Advertiser, 1795 to present

Staffordshire County Council Education Department 1969. *The Staffordshire Pottery Industry.* Local History Source Book 4. Staffordshire County Council, Stafford

Staffordshire Times 1876. Mr T Hughe's manufactory, Waterloo Road, Burslem. 22 July. Reprinted in Local History Pamphlet 16, HRL

Staffordshire Weekly Sentinel, 1919–25

Stanley, R 1845. Report on the state of Birmingham and other large towns. In *Second Report of the Commissioners for Inquiry into Large Towns with Popular Districts,* vol I. HMSO, London

Stoke-on-Trent Housing Committee 1960. *City of Stoke-on-Trent 1919–1960.* City Council, Stoke-on-Trent

Stoke-on-Trent Tenants Ltd c1913. *The Potteries Garden Village, Stoke-on-Trent. An Account of the Founding of the Penkhull Garden Village*

Stuart, D (ed) 1985. *People of the Potteries. A Dictionary of Local Biography,* vol I. Department of Adult Education, University of Keele

Swenarton, M 1981. *Homes Fit for Heroes. The Politics and Architecture of Early State Housing in Britain.* Heinemann Educational, London

Tait, H and Cherry, J 1978. Excavations at the Longton Hall porcelain factory. Part 1. *Post-Medieval Archaeology* **11**, 1–29

1980. Excavations at the Longton Hall porcelain factory. Part 2. *Post-Medieval Archaeology* **14**, 1–21

Talbot, R 1980. *Penkhull Remembered Again.* Cartwright Bros, Stoke-on-Trent

Tann, J 1970. *The Development of the Factory.* Cornmarket, London

Tarn, J N 1971. *Working-class Housing in Nineteenth-century Britain.* Architectural Association Paper No. 7. Lund Humphries, London

1973. *Five Per Cent Philanthropy. An Account of Housing in Urban Areas 1840–1914.* Cambridge University Press, Cambridge

Thomas, J 1971. *The Rise of the Staffordshire Potteries.* Adams and Dart, Somerset

Thompson, W J 1974. *Industrial Archaeology of North Staffordshire.* Moorland Publishing, Buxton

Townley, W E 1969. Urban administration and health; a case study of Hanley in the mid-nineteenth century. Unpublished MA thesis, University of Keele

Transactions British Ceramic Society (1915–16) **15**, 73 'Question box'

Tunstall 1816. Tunstall Building Society Articles of Agreement. William Salt Library, Stafford

1873. Tunstall Borough Board of Health Annual Reports

Turner, J B nd, c1974. Stokeville Building Society 1850–1856, and those who became involved in its project. Unpublished dissertation, University of Keele. Copy HRL

Turner, W (ed) 1904. *William Adams: an Old English Potter*. Chapman and Hall, London

Ure, A 1839. *A Dictionary of Arts, Manufacturers and Mines: Containing a Clear Exposition of Their Principles and Practice*, vol III. London. 7th edn 1878, Longmans, Green and Co, London

VCH 1963. *Staffordshire*, vol VIII. Oxford University Press, London

1967. *Staffordshire*, vol II. Oxford University Press, London

Warburton, W H 1931. *Trade Union Organisation in the North Staffordshire Potteries*. Allen and Unwin, London

Ward, J 1843. *The Borough of Stoke-upon-Trent*. W Lewis and Son, London. Reprinted 1984, Webberley, Stoke-on-Trent

Warrillow, E J D 1960. *A Sociological History of Stoke-on-Trent*. Etruscan Publications, Stoke-on-Trent

Weatherill, L 1971. *The Pottery Trade and North Staffordshire 1660–1760*. Manchester University Press

1981. The growth of the pottery industry in England 1660–1815. Unpublished PhD thesis, London School of Economics

Wedgwood, J C 1924–5. Court Rolls of the Manor of Tunstall. *NSFCT* **59**, 34–86

White, W 1851. *History, Gazetteer and Directory of Staffordshire*

Whiter, L 1970. *Spode*. Barrie and Jenkins, London

Willis-Fear, M J W 1965. The history of the pottery firm of W H Goss of Stoke-on-Trent. *Proceedings of the University of Newcastle-upon-Tyne Philosophical Society* **1** (4)

Winyard, E 1983. Etruria Hall. Research study of Etruria Hall and Works commissioned by the National Garden Festival, using Wedgwood MSS KUL. Unpublished, reproduced by KUL

MAPS

Allbut, T and Son, 1802. *Map of the Staffordshire Potteries*. SRO

Duchy of Lancaster, 1777. Plans of the encroachment and cottages, Hanley, Shelton and Penkhull. DL Private Collection

Duchy of Lancaster, 1812. Five maps of Hanley and Shelton showing mines. DL Private Collection

Duke of Sutherland. Various nineteenth-century estate plans, Trentham and Longton. SRO

Hargreaves, T, 1832. *Map of the Staffordshire Potteries*. SRO

Heaton, W, early nineteenth century. Copy of a plan of the town of Burslem, c1720. WSL

Homer, C J, 1857. Plan of the townships of Hanley and Shelton situated in the parish of Stoke-on-Trent. SRO

Malabar, R, 1848. Plan of the township of Tunstall. SRO

Ordnance Survey,   Staffordshire, HRL
    1851, 1871. *Burslem* 1:500
    1856, 1878. *Longton* 1:500
    1866, 1878. *Hanley* 1:500
    1878. *Stoke and Fenton* 1:500
    1878. *Tunstall* 1:500
    1878, 1900, 1912, 1924. *The Potteries* 1:2500

Tithe maps and awards 1839–50. All areas of the Potteries, LJRO, excepting Burslem and part of Wolstanton, SRO

Tithe redemption certificate 1828–59: individual plots, information and plans of various parts of Potteries. STKMG

Yates, W, 1775. *A Map of Staffordshire*. KUL

INDEX